THE HOLOCAUST LIBRARY

The Nazis

Lucent Books, P.O. Box 289011, San Diego, CA 92198-9011

Books in the Holocaust Library

THE HOLOCAUST LIBRARY

The Nazis

by

WILLIAM W. LACE

Library of Congress Cataloging-in-Publication Data

Lace, William W.
   The Nazis / by William W. Lace
      p. cm. — (The Holocaust library)
   Includes bibliographical references and index.
   Summary: A history of the Nazi movement in Germany beginning in 1919 with the German Workers' Party and including discussion of Adolf Hitler, anti-Semitism, and World War II.
   ISBN 1-56006-091-3 (alk. paper)
   1. Germany—History—1933–1945—Juvenile literature. 2. National socialism—Juvenile literature. 3. Hitler, Adolf, 1889–1945—Juvenile literature. [1. Germany—History—1933–1945. 2. National socialism. 3. Hitler, Adolf, 1889–1945.] I. Title. II. Series: Holocaust library (San Diego, Calif.)
DD256.5.L32   1998
943.086—dc21

                                        97-21376
                                         CIP
                                         AC

Table of Contents

Foreword

More than eleven million innocent people, mostly Jews but also millions of others deemed "subhuman" by Adolf Hitler such as Gypsies, Russians, and Poles, were murdered by the Germans during World War II. The magnitude and unique horror of the Holocaust continues to make it a focal point in history—not only the history of modern times, but also the entire record of humankind. While the war itself temporarily changed the political landscape, the Holocaust forever changed the way we look at ourselves.

Starting with the European Renaissance in the 1400s, continuing through the Enlightenment of the 1700s, and extending to the Liberalism of the 1800s, philosophers and others developed the idea that people's intellect and reason allowed them to rise above their animal natures and conquer poverty, brutality, warfare, and all manner of evils. Given the will to do so, there was no height to which humanity might not rise. Was not mankind, these people argued, the noblest creation of God—in the words of the Bible, "a little lower than the angels"?

Western Europeans believed so heartily in these concepts that when rumors of mass murders by the Nazis began to emerge, people refused to accept—despite mounting evidence—that such things could take place. Even the Jews who were being deported to the death camps had a hard time believing that they were headed toward extermination. Rational beings, they argued, could not commit such actions. When the veil of secrecy was finally ripped from the death camps, however, the world recoiled in shock and horror. If humanity was capable of such depravity, what was its true nature? Were humans lower even than animals instead of just beneath the angels?

The perpetration of the Holocaust, so far outside the bounds of society's experience, cried out for explanations. For more than a half century, people have sought them. Thousands of books, diaries, sermons, poems, plays, films, and lectures have been devoted to almost every imaginable aspect of the Holocaust, yet it remains one of the most difficult episodes in history to understand.

Some scholars have explained the Holocaust as a uniquely German event, pointing to the racial supremacy theories of German philosophers, the rigidity of German society, and the tradition of obedience to authority. Others have seen it as a uniquely Jewish phenomenon, the culmination of centuries of anti-Semitism in Christian Europe. Still others have said that the Holocaust was a unique combination of these two factors—a set of circumstances unlikely ever to recur.

Such explanations are comfortable and simple—too simple. The Holocaust was neither a German event nor a Jewish event. It was a human event. The same forces—racism, prejudice, fanaticism—that sent millions to the gas chambers have not disappeared. If anything, they have become more evident. One cannot say, "It can't happen again." On a different scale, it has happened again. More than a million Cambodians were killed between 1974 and 1979 by a Communist government. In 1994 thousands of innocent civilians were murdered in tribal warfare between the Hutu and Tutsi tribes in the African nations of Burundi and Rwanda. Christian Serbs in Bosnia embarked on a program of "ethnic cleansing" in the mid-1990s, seeking to rid the country of Muslims.

The complete answer to the Holocaust has proved elusive. Indeed, it may never be found. The search, however, must continue. As author Elie Wiesel, a survivor of the death camps, wrote, "No one has the right to speak for the dead. . . . Still, the story had to be told. In spite of all risks, all possible misunderstandings. It needed to be told for the sake of our children."

Each book in Lucent Books' seven volume Holocaust Library covers a different topic that reveals the full gamut of human response to the Holocaust. *The Nazis*, *The Final Solution*, *The Death Camps* and *Nazi War Criminals* focus on the perpetrators of the Holocaust and their plan to eliminate the Jewish people. Volumes on *The Righteous Gentiles*, *The Resistance*, and *The Survivors* reveal that humans are capable of being the noblest creation of God—people can still commit acts of bravery and altruism even in the most terrible circumstances.

History offers a way to interpret and reinterpret the past and an opportunity to alter the future. Lucent Books' topic-centered approach is an ideal introduction for students to study such phenomena as the Holocaust. After all, only by becoming knowledgeable about such atrocities can humanity hope to prevent future crimes from occurring. Although such historical lessons seem clear and unavoidable, as historian Yehuda Bauer wrote, "People seldom learn from history. Can we be an exception?"

Chronology of Events

1919

January 2 German Workers' Party founded in Munich by Karl Harrer and Anton Drexler

September 19 Adolf Hitler joins German Workers' Party

1920

February 24 Hitler outlines German Workers' Party platform in speech in Munich

March German Workers' Party changes name to National Socialist German Workers' Party, soon becomes known as Nazi Party

1923

Summer Hitler establishes *Sturmabteilung* (SA), puts down inner-party dissent, becomes absolute leader of Nazis

Fall Hitler establishes *Stabswache*, forerunner of SS

November 8–9 Beer Hall Putsch in Munich fails

November 11 Hitler arrested and imprisoned

1924

February 24 Hitler and other Nazi leaders tried for high treason

April 1 Hitler sentenced to five years in prison, begins to write *Mein Kampf*

May 4 First Nazis elected to German Reichstag

December 7 Nazis lose ground in national elections

December 20 Hitler released from prison on parole

1925

February 24 Nazi Party, banned after Beer Hall Putsch, re-forms in Munich

1927

July 14 First volume of *Mein Kampf* published

August 19 First Nazi Party rally in Nuremberg

1928

May 20 Nazis receive 2.5 percent of vote in Reichstag elections

1929

January 6 Heinrich Himmler made head of SS

1930

February Murdered storm trooper Horst Wessel cultivated as martyr by Nazis

March Heinrich Brüning replaces Herman Müller as chancellor of Germany

September 2 Hitler assumes supreme leadership of SA

September 14 Nazis gain 18 percent of vote in Reichstag elections

December 31 SS establishes Central Office for Race and Resettlement

1931

September 18 Hitler's niece, Geli Raubal, found shot to death

October 10 Hitler's first meeting with Paul von Hindenburg

1932

February 25 Hitler takes German citizenship

March 13 Hitler finishes strong second to Hindenburg in presidential election

April 10 Hindenburg defeats Hitler in runoff election for presidency

April 14 Chancellor Brüning bans SA and SS

May 30 Brüning resigns as chancellor, replaced by Franz von Papen

June 16 Papen lifts ban on SA and SS

July 31 Nazis achieve majority in Reichstag

1933

January 30 Hitler appointed chancellor

February 27 Fire destroys Reichstag building

February 28 Hitler given emergency powers to suspend civil liberties

March 13 Joseph Goebbels made minister for public enlightenment and propaganda

March 23 Reichstag passes Enabling Act giving Hitler absolute power

April 1 Nationwide boycott of Jewish businesses

April 7 First anti-Jewish laws passed by Reichstag

April 26 *Geheime Staatspolizei* (Gestapo) established

July 14 Nazis declared sole political party in Germany

October 14 Germany withdraws from international disarmament conference

1934

January 26 Hitler announces nonaggression treaty with Poland

March *Sicherheitsdienst* (SD) formed

June 30 Hitler's opponents killed in Blood Purge

July 20 SS made independent of SA

August 2 Hindenburg dies; Hitler combines offices of president and chancellor, becoming führer of Germany; military officers required to pledge personal loyalty to Hitler

1935

January 13 Citizens of the Saar vote overwhelmingly to be made part of Germany

March 16 Hitler announces military draft; formation of Luftwaffe

September 13 Nuremberg Laws strip Jews of rights as citizens

1936

March 7 German troops reoccupy the Rhineland

Summer Olympic Games held in Berlin; anti-Jewish activity halted

September 9 Four-Year Plan announced

October 21 Germany, Italy sign treaty of cooperation

1937

January 30 Hitler declares Treaty of Versailles void

1938

March Germany annexes Austria

September 29–30 Britain, France cede Czech Sudetenland to Germany in Munich agreement

November 9–10 SS mobs destroy Jewish shops, synagogues in *Kristallnacht* riots

1939

March 31 British government announces unconditional support of Poland

May 22 Italy, Germany sign "Pact of Steel" military alliance

May 23 Hitler informs military leaders that war with Poland is "inevitable"

August 23 Germany, Soviet Union sign nonaggression pact in Moscow

September 1 Germany invades Poland

September 3 France, Britain declare war on Germany

October 12 All Jews evacuated from Vienna

1940

February 12 Beginning of evacuation of Jews from Germany

May 10 Germany attacks France, Belgium, the Netherlands, Luxembourg

June 21 France signs surrender to Germany at Compiègne

August 13 Battle of Britain begins

1941

June 22 Germany invades Soviet Union

December 4 Soviet army launches counterattack near Moscow

December 7 Japan attacks U.S. naval base at Pearl Harbor

December 11 Germany declares war on United States

December 19 Hitler assumes personal command of all German armed forces

1942

January 20 Conference at Wannsee outside Berlin decides on extermination as the "final solution" to the "Jewish problem"

June 23 Full-scale gassings begin at Auschwitz

October 4 All Jews in concentration camps ordered sent to Auschwitz

November 5 German troops in North Africa defeated by British in Battle of El Alamein

November 19 Russians launch counteroffensive against Germans at Stalingrad

1943

February 2 Russians recapture Stalingrad

September 3 Allied troops land in Italy

1944

September 20 Hitler injured in assassination attempt by Klaus von Stauffenberg

June 6 D day: Allied troops land on beaches of Normandy in France

1945

January 14 East Prussia invaded by Russian troops

March 7 American troops cross the Rhine River into Germany

April 13 Vienna occupied by Russian troops

April 20 Top Nazi leaders gather for last time

April 23 Russian troops reach outskirts of Berlin

April 25 Allies refuse Himmler's offer to surrender SS

April 28 Benito Mussolini executed

April 30 Hitler commits suicide in underground bunker in Berlin

May 2 Fall of Berlin to Russians

May 7 General Alfred Jodl signs unconditional German surrender

May 9 Göring captured by American soldiers

May 23 Himmler commits suicide after capture by British

November 20 Top Nazis go on trial in Nuremberg

1946

October 15 Göring commits suicide in prison

October 16 Nine top Nazis hanged in Nuremberg prison

Before the Storm

Any study of the Nazis should begin with two questions. First, what aspects of German character and German history permitted them to gain control of a modern nation? Second, why were the Jews the special objects of the Nazis' hatred, targeted by them for extermination?

The answer to the second question—why the Jews?—goes back almost to the beginning of recorded history. About 1200 B.C., the Jews of Palestine developed a strict set of laws and a belief in a single God, a belief that set them apart from all other people in the region. Despite persecution, they held fast to their religion, laws, and culture. Eventually, in A.D. 135, they were driven from their homeland by the Romans.

From this time until the foundation of modern Israel in 1948, the Jews were without a homeland. Wherever they lived, they were a people apart, observing their own religious laws and customs. They were everywhere the strangers, the outsiders. Many Christians claimed that the Jews should be held eternally responsible for Jesus' crucifixion. They were accused of using the blood of Christian babies in their rituals. In the Middle Ages, some European countries, including England and Spain, expelled the Jews.

One reason the Jews were not banished from Germany was that there was no Germany. Instead, Germany was a collection of

When German Jews rejected the teachings of Martin Luther, the Reformation leader became a notorious anti-Semite. His hatred of the Jews was passed on to later generations of Germans.

virtually independent states. In the absence of a formal national policy of persecution, the Jews were able to survive—although in constant fear—in hundreds of isolated communities. They might have remained there largely unmolested had it not been for the man who was probably the most influential German in history—Martin Luther.

Luther brought about great reforms in Christianity, but he was a disaster for the Jews. At first, he reached out to them, expecting their support of what he held to be the true meaning of Christianity—absolute faith in Jesus as a savior. When they rejected his teaching, however, he became violently anti-Jewish. Through his influence, anti-Jewish feeling became a fixture of German culture. As Holocaust historian John Weiss writes, Luther "struck a powerful chord in the souls of millions of peasants and artisans of Northern Germany, a chord echoing down to the twentieth century."[1]

The "Subhuman" Race

Especially ominous was Luther's view that the Jews were beyond salvation. "I cannot convert the Jews," he wrote. "Our Lord Christ Himself did not succeed in doing so; but I can close their mouths so that there will be nothing for them to do but lie upon the ground."[2] To Luther and his followers, Jews had no souls and were less than human. The ultimate expression of this view—that the Jews were a subhuman species to be exterminated—would later be adopted by the Nazis.

In more modern times, while other European countries slowly moved toward democratic forms of government, Germany remained a patchwork of small principalities, each with an absolute ruler. Not only were any liberalizing influences suppressed, but the German tradition of obedience to

authority, as preached by Luther, was strengthened. While Jews in other parts of Europe benefited from a new climate of toleration, those in Germany remained the targets of unremitting hate.

In the 1800s, the Germans rejected the central tenets of the intellectual movement known as the Enlightenment, which taught that people's beliefs are shaped exclusively by rational observation and experiment. German philosophers instead took the traditional view that people are guided chiefly by an inner spirit. Furthermore, they said, the most pure form of the human spirit was found in the Germans.

In the second half of the 1800s, the Germans used or perverted the writing of Charles Darwin to develop scientific support for the idea of a German super race. Darwin wrote that in a process he termed natural selection, species passed on certain advantageous traits to future generations. This theory of the "survival of the fittest" was later applied to ethnic groups as Social Darwinism, the idea that competition among humans is a natural process and that the strongest group should rule.

In Germany, Social Darwinism led to the concept of the *Völk*, a German word meaning people, but in a tribal sense. The *Völk* were united by blood, and the most pure blood supposedly was that of the ancestors of the Germans, a Caucasian, northern European people known as the Aryans. It was the destiny of the *Völk* to cleanse itself of impure blood, maintain its racial purity, and create a *völkisch* state that would rule the world.

The archenemies of the *Völk*, in the eyes of German philosophers, were the Jews, corrupters of pure Aryan blood. Wilhelm Marr wrote in 1879 that the Jews were out to achieve world domination at the expense of the *Völk*. It was not the religion of the

Jews that posed a threat, he wrote, but their inborn and unchangeable racial traits. Marr invented the term *anti-Semitism* to indicate that the Jews should be opposed on racial rather than religious grounds. This was an important distinction: To future generations, it was the Jews themselves, not their religion, that should be stamped out.

The Rise of Prussia

German unity was finally achieved in 1871 through the expansion of the kingdom of Prussia, a highly militarized state based on rigid discipline and obedience to authority. Prussia's rise to power was largely the work of Chancellor Otto von Bismarck, a hater of democracy who said, "The great questions of the day will not be settled by resolutions and majority votes . . . but by blood and iron."[3]

Within ten years of Bismarck's taking office, Prussia had brought all the German states under its rule and was the greatest power on the European continent. The Prussian king was proclaimed kaiser, or emperor, of Germany, ruler of the Second Reich, or empire. The First Reich had been the medieval Holy Roman Empire. The Third Reich would be Nazi Germany.

The new, unified Germany was determined to take its place among the world's great powers. The other great European powers, Great Britain and France, tried to limit Germany's influence, and the rivalry finally erupted in 1914 into the conflict known as World War I.

The war lasted four years and left more

Otto von Bismarck led Prussia's rise to power and its eventual takeover of all of the independent states of Germany.

than 8 million dead. In November 1918 the German army knew victory was impossible. The generals, led by Field Marshal Paul von Hindenburg, convinced the kaiser to relinquish his crown. They then agreed to a civilian government, which they advised to sign an armistice with the victorious Allies. Later, German generals would claim the war could have been won and that the army had been "stabbed in the back" by what they called the "November criminals"[4]—liberals, Communists, and Jews.

The defeat of Germany came as a profound shock to the German people. Even

Demonstrators protest the conditions imposed on Germany after its defeat in World War I. The Treaty of Versailles not only forced the Germans to take sole responsibility for the war, but also to make huge reparation payments that virtually guaranteed the continued ruin of the German economy.

more shocking were the terms of the Treaty of Versailles that ended the war. Germany lost more than a third of her territory and all her colonies. Most of her weapons and ships were to be surrendered to the Allies. Worst of all, Germany was to pay the staggering sum of $35 billion for property damages done by the war and admit sole responsibility for causing the war, a provision that humiliated and rankled the German people.

The Weimar Constitution

In 1919 a National Assembly made up mostly of liberal and moderate politicians met in the city of Weimar to draw up a new constitution. The Weimar Constitution, an excellent model, would fail chiefly because the German people wanted it to. The extreme liberals wished to institute a socialist or Soviet-style Communist government. The extreme conservatives wanted a more authoritarian government, perhaps even to return to a monarchy. Most ordinary Germans, with their history of obedience to authority, feared and distrusted democracy.

Postwar Germany was a shambles. The people were embittered and discouraged. The economy was a wreck. Inflation rose to such absurd levels that a postage stamp cost 5 billion deutsche marks. Communists threatening to topple the Weimar Republic battled the *Freikorps*, or Free Corps, gangs of former professional soldiers hired by the government. More than forty political parties formed and re-formed in coalitions that accomplished little or nothing. The opportunity was ripe for a strong leader, someone who would take control, bring order, and restore Germany to prominence. Such a leader came forward. His name was Adolf Hitler.

Der Führer

Dozens of political parties vied for power in the chaos that was Germany following World War I. Although some had large followings, none was able to gain a majority in the Reichstag, Germany's legislature. Most were small, and one of the smallest was the *Deutsche Arbeiterpartei*, or German Workers' Party, later to become the Nazi Party. That this tiny group of malcontents should evolve into a force that would threaten to conquer the world was due to the twisted genius of one man—Adolf Hitler.

Hitler, the man who would lead Germany to the heights of conquest and the depths of total defeat, was not even a German. He was born on April 20, 1889, in the Austrian town of Braunau am Inn near the German border, the third child of Alois Hitler, a minor customs official, and his third wife, Klara Pölzl.

In his autobiography and political testament, *Mein Kampf* (*My Struggle*), Hitler claimed he had grown up in poverty. This was not true. Alois Hitler had done well in government service. He retired in 1895 with a comfortable pension and settled in the village of Leonding near the town of Linz. However, while Adolf Hitler's childhood was far from poor, it was also far from happy. Alois Hitler was a bitter, ill-tempered

man who, in his mid-fifties, had little time for or patience with his son. Adolf's mother, on the other hand, smothered him with attention and would later make excuses for his failures.

Hitler as an infant. Although Hitler's mother spoiled her only son, later in life Hitler had little time for his mother, not even visiting her when she was on her deathbed.

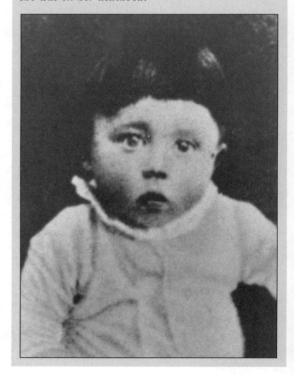

Hitler later claimed that he and his father argued over his future career, his father wanting him to enter civil service and Adolf determined to become an artist. Since Alois Hitler died in 1903, well before Adolf was old enough to embark on a career, their quarrels probably centered on something else, namely Adolf's poor performance in school. He had high marks in drawing and gymnastics but barely passed history and geography and failed German, mathematics, and shorthand. He apparently had a quick mind but was unwilling to study and quickly lost interest in most subjects. One of his teachers, Dr. Edward Huemer, later recalled:

He had definite talent, though in a narrow field. But he lacked self-discipline, being notoriously cantankerous, willful, arrogant, and bad-tempered. He had obvious difficulty in fitting in at school. Moreover he was lazy . . . his enthusiasm for hard work evaporated all too quickly. He reacted with ill-concealed hostility to advice or reproof; at the same time, he demanded of his fellow pupils their unqualified subservience, fancying himself in the role of a leader.[5]

Blaming Others

Hitler blamed his failure at school on everything but himself. Above all, he blamed his teachers, calling them

absolute tyrants. They had no sympathy with youth; their one object was to stuff our brains and turn us into erudite apes like themselves. If any pupil showed the slightest trace of originality, they persecuted him relentlessly, and the only model pupils whom I have ever got to know have all been failures in after-life.[6]

Hitler would display many of these same traits, blaming others for his own mistakes and reacting violently to any form of criticism. His failure in school left him with a deep-seated feeling of inferiority that drove him to exhibit superiority over those with more education and experience, even in areas in which he was unqualified to do so.

Only one teacher made an impression on Hitler, but it would be an impression of lasting importance. His history teacher, Dr. Leopold Poetsch, was an ardent German nationalist who impressed his vision of German destiny on his young pupil. Hitler later wrote,

There we [Hitler and his classmates] sat, often aflame with enthusiasm, sometimes even moved to tears. . . . He used our budding national fanaticism as a means of educating us, frequently appealing to our sense of national honor . . . though he had no such intention, it was then that I became a young revolutionary.[7]

Hitler left school in 1905 at the age of sixteen, without graduating, and spent the next two years living in idleness with his devoted mother. Although relatives urged him to get a job to help with family expenses, he dreamed only of becoming an artist or architect. He spent his days drawing or walking around Linz, envisioning the grand changes he would make. He once talked his only friend, August Kubizek, into pooling their money to buy a lottery ticket. With the winnings, they would rent a mansion in which Hitler would study art and Kubizek music. Their studio would be presided over by Stephanie, a beautiful girl Hitler followed around Linz but was too shy to address.

Hitler the Reader

Those who knew Adolf Hitler as a youth and a young man recalled the extent to which he read books. In this passage from *Mein Kampf,* quoted in William Shirer's *The Rise and Fall of the Third Reich*, Hitler describes his reading habits. They lead one to suspect that Hitler did not so much learn from what he read as he used his reading to strengthen the views he already held.

During this time [1909–1913] I read enormously and thoroughly. All the free time my work left me was employed in my studies. In this way I forged in a few years' time the foundations of a knowledge from which I still draw nourishment today. . . . By "reading," to be sure, I mean perhaps something different than the average member of our so-called "intelligentsia." I know of people who "read" enormously . . . yet whom I would not describe as "well-read." True, they possess a mass of "knowledge," but their brain is unable to organize and register the material they have taken in. . . . On the other hand, a man who possesses the art of correct reading will . . . instinctively and immediately perceive everything which in his opinion is worth permanently remembering, either because it is suited to his purpose or generally worth knowing. . . . The art of reading, as of learning, is this: . . . to *retain the essential, to forget the nonessential*. . . . Only this kind of reading has meaning and purpose.

Hitler's Dream World

Hitler was living in a dream world. His visions went beyond the ordinary fantasies of a teenager; to Hitler, they were real. When he failed to win the lottery, Kubizek later wrote, Hitler reacted violently, blaming "the entire social order."[8] All his life, Hitler would have trouble telling reality from fantasy.

When he was not walking with Kubizek, Hitler was in the local library reading. "It was always books and more books," Kubizek wrote. "I cannot imagine Adolf without books. At home he would have them piled up all round him. If he was really interested in a book he always had to have it with him. . . . Books were his whole world."[9] Among the authors Hitler read was Friedrich Nietzsche, and there can be little doubt that the young man eagerly absorbed the German philosopher's theories of a super race.

The two years in Linz should have been carefree years for Hitler, but he was constantly tormented by feelings that the entire world was against him. "He saw everywhere only obstacles and hostility," Kubizek wrote. "He was always up against something and at odds with the world."[10]

Hitler first visited the Austrian capital of Vienna in 1906; he was entranced by its majestic buildings and the splendor of its art galleries and opera houses. Deciding to enter Vienna's Academy of Fine Arts, in 1907 Hitler talked his mother into giving him a portion of his inheritance, then, though his mother was ill with breast cancer, left her in Linz and went to Vienna to live the life of a student.

He took the entrance examination to the Academy in October 1907 and was rejected. It was a terrible blow to Hitler, who had convinced himself that he had

Hitler's rendering of a British estate reveals a limited talent. It is interesting to wonder what course Hitler's life would have taken if he had been accepted to art school and fulfilled his artistic dreams.

great talent. He vowed to stay in Vienna, even though his mother was dying, to improve his drawing technique and to retake the examination.

Hitler lived in Vienna the next year, sharing an apartment with his friend Kubizek, who was studying music. After his mother died in December 1907, he received the remainder of his inheritance and began to spend it on books, sightseeing, opera, and in coffeehouses. According to Kubizek, he did very little drawing.

In July 1908 Kubizek returned to Linz for the summer, expecting to rejoin his friend in the fall. When he returned, Hitler had disappeared. He had tried once more in September to enter the Academy, but this time he was not even permitted to take the exam. He turned toward architecture but discovered that his failure to graduate from high school barred him from that career. His dream world shattered, his money all but gone, he buried himself in Vienna's slums.

The Vagrant in Vienna

For the next five years, 1909–1913, Adolf Hitler, later one of the most powerful men on earth, was a down-and-out vagrant in the back streets of Vienna. He had squandered his inheritance and lived on an orphan's pension too small to buy food. In warm weather, he slept in doorways or on park benches. Winter weather drove him indoors to shelters for the homeless. Later, those who remembered Hitler during those years recalled a thin, pale, unshaven youth who wore a shabby, secondhand overcoat and a greasy derby hat covering hair that came down over a dirty shirt collar.

Even after his rejection by the Academy of Fine Arts, he held on to his dream—by now a fantasy—of becoming an artist. He refused to look for steady work, instead making a little money selling small paintings, mostly of Viennese landmarks. He was frequently broke and always hungry. In *Mein Kampf* he wrote, "Hunger was then my faithful bodyguard; he never left me for a moment and partook of all I had. . . . My life was a continual struggle with this pitiless friend."[11]

The daily struggle to survive hardened Hitler. "The idea of struggle is as old as life itself, for life is only preserved because other living things perish through struggle. . . . In this struggle, the stronger, the more able, win, while the less able, the weak, lose,"[12] he later said. Many in his position would have been drawn to socialism or communism, but Hitler looked with disgust on ordinary workers as weak and powerless. Moreover, his passionate German nationalism would not allow him to embrace any philosophy that preached

Enemy of the Working Class

Although the term *Nazi* was a shortened version of the German *Nationalsozialistische*, or National Socialists, the party was anything but socialist in outlook. Hitler never identified with any movement or ideology that proposed control of the government by the working classes or any kind of international unity of workers. In *Mein Kampf*, as quoted in Allan Bullock's *Hitler: A Study in Tyranny*, Hitler described how he viewed socialists during his days in Vienna:

All that I heard had the effect of arousing the strongest antagonism in me. Everything was disparaged—the nation because it was held to be an invention of the capitalist class (how often I had to listen to that phrase!); the Fatherland [Germany], because it was held to be an instrument in the hand of the bourgeoisie [the upper middle class] for the exploitation of the working masses; the authority of the law, because this was a means of holding down the proletariat [workers]; religion, as a means of doping the people, so as to exploit them afterwards; morality, as a badge of stupid and sheepish docility [meekness]. There was nothing that they did not drag in the mud. . . . Then I asked myself: are these men worthy to belong to a great people? The question was profoundly disturbing; for if the answer were "Yes", then the struggle to defend one's nationality is no longer worth all the trouble and sacrifice we demand of our best elements if it be in the interest of such a rabble. On the other hand, if the answer had to be "No", then our nation is poor indeed in men. During these days of mental anguish and deep meditation I saw before my mind the ever-increasing and menacing army of people who could no longer be reckoned as belonging to their own nation.

universal brotherhood. To Hitler, the world belonged to the strong and heroic, and any theory that said otherwise, such as communism, was "a pestilential whore covered with the mask of social virtue and brotherly love."[13]

Hitler also developed his irrational, pathological hatred for Jews during this period. Until then, he had had relatively little contact with Jews, but Vienna in 1910 was one-tenth Jewish, and many of the Jews, especially those from eastern Europe, lived in the poor sections where Hitler saw them daily. One day, he later wrote,

> I suddenly encountered an apparition in a black caftan [a kind of full-length overcoat] and black sidelocks [of hair]. Is this a Jew? was my first thought. For, to be sure, they had not looked like that in Linz. I observed the man furtively and cautiously, but the longer I stared at this foreign face, scrutinizing feature for feature, the more my first question assumed a new form: Is this a German?[14]

The Jewish "Threat"

To Hitler and to millions of others steeped in German anti-Semitism, the answer was a violent no. The Jews were foreign and alien; they could never be German. Their very presence was a threat to German purity. This came as a profound awakening to Hitler. He began to read anti-Semitic literature, much of which reviled Jews in sordid, pornographic terms. He came to believe that Jews were at the bottom of everything wrong with society. "Was there any form of filth or profligacy [extravagance], particularly in cultural life, without at least one Jew involved in it?" he wrote. "If you cut even cautiously into such an abscess, you find, like a maggot in a rotting body, often dazzled by the sudden light—a little Jew."[15]

Such ravings went far beyond mere prejudice. Historian Klaus Fischer writes, "It was a psychopathology of the sort that must be ranked with witchcraft and demonology in the history of the human race."[16] In other words, Hitler's anti-Semitism sprang not from any intellectual reasoning or political philosophy but from his own, deeply disturbed personality. Up until now, his irrational fears and accusations had been directed everywhere. In Vienna, they became focused on the Jews. "I finally discovered who were the evil sprits leading our people astray," he wrote.[17]

Hitler made other discoveries in Vienna that he would later put to use. Although he despised its philosophy, he appreciated the methods of the liberal Social Democratic Party. He attended its rallies. He studied its leaders' speeches. In *Mein Kampf* he wrote what was to be a blueprint for Nazi propaganda and terror:

> I understood the infamous spiritual terror which this movement exerts. . . . At a given sign it unleashes a veritable barrage of lies and slanders against whatever adversary seems most dangerous. . . . This is a tactic based on precise calculation of all human weakness, and its result will lead to success with almost mathematical certainty. . . . I achieved an equal understanding of the importance of physical terror toward the individual and the masses. . . . For while in the ranks of their supporters the victory achieved seems a triumph of the justice of their own cause, the defeated adversary in most cases despairs of the success of any further resistance.[18]

The Munich Years

In 1913 Hitler left Vienna for Munich, the capital of the German state of Bavaria. He

Was Hitler Part Jewish?

Suspicions surfaced during Hitler's lifetime that he might have had a Jewish grandfather, his ancestry on his father's side being unclear. His paternal grandmother was Maria Schicklgruber, who in 1837 returned, unmarried and pregnant, from her job as a housemaid in Graz to her native village. Her son was born that year and christened Alois Schicklgruber. The space for the name of the father was left blank.

Five years later, Maria married Johann Georg Heidler, a wandering miller and the man presumed to be Alois's father. Heidler, however, did not take the trouble to have Alois's birth legitimized. Only when he was nearly forty years old did Alois change his name at the urging of his uncle, Johann Nepomuk Heidler, with whom he had lived as a boy. Johann Nepomuk Heidler swore an oath that his brother, now dead, was the father of Alois. The name was changed on the birth register but was misspelled as "Hitler."

The mystery is important because of the possibility that Alois Hitler's father was not Johann Georg Heidler, but the son of a Jewish family in Graz named Frankenberger for whom Maria had worked at the time her son was conceived. This would explain why Heidler never acknowledged his son. In 1930 Adolf Hitler learned of the possibility that he had a Jewish grandfather and asked a Nazi lawyer, Hans Frank, to investigate. Frank, according to his biography, written as he was awaiting execution after World War II and quoted by Klaus Fischer in *Nazi Germany: A New History*, told Hitler that "starting on the day the child [Alois] was born and continuing right up to its fourteenth year, Frankenberger Senior paid maintenance to the mother on behalf of his [Frankenberger's] nineteen-year-old son." If Adolf Hitler, who by 1930 had made anti-Semitism a cornerstone of Nazism, suspected he himself was one-quarter Jewish, it might have triggered his determination to eradicate all Jews in order to cover up his secret.

---

probably left to avoid military service, not because he was a coward but because he hated the thought of being in an army that would include all the ethnic groups of Austria-Hungary, including "everywhere the eternal mushroom of humanity—Jews."[19] He wrote later that his months in Munich were "the happiest time of my life."[20]

On August 1, 1914, as Germany went to war against France and England, Hitler joined a cheering, singing crowd in a Munich plaza. His life now had a purpose! He would help carry Germany to victory and world domination. Two days later he applied as a volunteer in the German army, even though he was an Austrian citizen. He was inducted and ten weeks later found himself at the battle line in France.

Hitler served as a courier carrying dispatches and orders between the front lines and the regimental headquarters in the rear. His bravery in battle is unquestioned. He was wounded twice and decorated twice, the second time with the Iron Cross First Class, a medal seldom given to an enlisted man and the only one Hitler ever wore.

Though brave and competent, Hitler was not popular with his fellow soldiers. He was promoted to corporal but rose no higher. He kept apart from others, making no friends, receiving no mail. One member of his regiment wrote that Hitler was

> a peculiar fellow. He sat in the corner of our mess [dining hall] holding his head between his hands, in deep contemplation. Suddenly he would leap up, and, running about excitedly, say that in spite of our big guns, victory would be denied us, for the invisible foes of the German people [the Jews] were a greater danger than the biggest cannon of the enemy.[21]

A Fateful Decision

In Hitler's last battle on October 13, 1918, he was caught in a gas attack and almost blinded. He was recovering in a hospital near Berlin when an army chaplain brought the news that Germany had surrendered. Another of Hitler's dreams had exploded. He was overcome with grief. Germany had not been defeated, he thought, but betrayed by liberal politicians and, above all, by the Jews. As he lay in his hospital bed, he vowed to avenge the wrongs done to his adopted country. "My own fate became known to me," he wrote. "I decided to go into politics."[22]

Hitler returned to a severely restricted postwar army whose officers were determined to resist the democracy that was being forced on Germany. In 1919, when someone in a political instruction class spoke favorably of the Jews, Hitler jumped

Hitler (right) poses with his comrades during World War I. Hitler excelled as a soldier and was awarded the Iron Cross First Class for his bravery in battle.

up and delivered a violently anti-Semitic speech. His officers were impressed and assigned him to an educational unit in which he was offered "an opportunity of speaking before a larger audience; and the thing that I had always presumed from pure feeling without knowing it was now corroborated: I could speak."[23]

Hitler's duties also involved the investigation of the many political groups springing up throughout Bavaria. In September 1919 he received orders to attend a meeting

Hitler's oratory skills prompted the German Workers' Party to extend an invitation of membership. With this move, Hitler went from discontented vagrant to political activist.

of the *Deutsche Arbeiterpartei* (DAP). Despite its grand name, meaning German Workers' Party, the DAP was only one of several tiny right-wing groups. Toward the end of a rather dull round of speeches, one speaker suggested that Bavaria break off from Germany and join Austria. Hitler rose and spoke passionately about the need for all Germans to unite as a single nation.

The next day Hitler was surprised to receive an invitation to join the party. His first impulse was to decline. He wanted to create his own group, not join another. But he attended a meeting of the party's central committee and, even though bored with the trivial issues discussed there, was attracted to the small group. "After two days of agonized pondering and reflection," he later wrote, "I finally came to the conviction that I had to take this step. It was the most decisive resolve of my life. From here there was and could be no turning back."[24]

The next day Adolf Hitler became the seventh member of the board of the DAP. The thirty-year-old former vagrant had found the vehicle through which he would impose his radical views across two continents. The small party—soon to be known as the Nazis—had found its führer, the leader who would make the party's name synonymous with the Holocaust.

Birth of the Party

The German Workers' Party in 1919 hardly seemed a threat to the government of Bavaria, much less Germany, very much less the entire world. Four years later, however, through organization and terror tactics, it had developed into a major force in southern Germany. And Adolf Hitler, who had made himself the party führer, or absolute leader, was already surrounded by some of the men who would later play key roles in the Holocaust.

The wave of nationalism and anti-Semitism that swept Germany in the late 1800s led to the formation of many organizations dedicated to German superiority. One such group was the Thule Society. Although it presented itself to the outside world as a literary club, the Thule Society was a pulpit for extremists who preached the necessity of keeping German, or Aryan, blood pure so that, as a master race, Germans could take control of the world from their archenemies, the Jews. It received financial support from several wealthy and influential people in Bavaria.

In October 1918, seeking to expand its influence to the working class, the society instructed one of its members, journalist Karl Harrer, to merge his Political Workers' Circle with a small group called the Free Workers' Committee. This group, made up of twenty-five railroad workers, had been founded the previous March by Anton Drexler, a mechanic. The two groups met on January 2, 1919, and emerged as the German Workers' Party. It was this group that Hitler was to join later in the year.

Bavaria, and Munich in particular, were at that time fertile fields for right-wing groups of all kinds. In January 1919—about the same time the German Workers' Party was formed—a Communist government had taken control in the state. Led by three Russian Jews, the new government tried to eliminate right-wing opposition, throwing the leaders in prison. On May 1, a combination of army and Free Corps troops entered Munich and overthrew the Communists, killing many of the leaders.

These upheavals had three serious consequences. First, they aroused in the people a great loathing and dread of communism. From this time on, the sympathies of the vast majority of the German people were with right-wing groups. Second, they tended to solidify hatred of the Jews, many of whom had been leaders in the socialist and Communist movements. Third, they established that the real power in Germany remained with the army and the Free Corps with which they were closely allied. All three factors would make it easier for the DAP and similar groups to flourish.

Race as All-Important

National boundaries meant nothing to Hitler and the Nazis. To them, a nation was defined by the "blood" of its people, and the most pure form of blood was that of the German *Völk*. In this passage from Hermann Rauschning's *Hitler Speaks*, quoted in Allan Bullock's *Hitler: A Study in Tyranny*, the Nazi leader explains his idea of nationalism.

> The concept of the nation has become meaningless. We have to get rid of this false conception and set in its place the conception of race. The New Order cannot be conceived in terms of the national boundaries of the peoples with an historic past, but in terms of race that transcend these boundaries. . . . I know perfectly well that in the scientific sense there is no such thing as race. But you, as a farmer, cannot get your breeding right without the conception of race. And I, as a politician, need a conception which enables the order that has hitherto existed on an historic basis to be abolished, and an entirely new and anti-historic order enforced and given an intellectual basis. . . . And for this purpose the conception of race serves me well. . . . France carried her great Revolution beyond her borders with the conception of the nation. With the conception of race, National Socialism will carry its revolution abroad and recast the world. I shall bring into operation throughout all Europe and the whole world this process of selection which we have carried out through National Socialism in Germany. . . . The active sections in nations, the militant, Nordic section, will rise again and become the ruling element over these shopkeepers and pacifists, these puritans and speculators and busybodies. . . . There will not be much left then of the clichés of nationalism, and precious little among us Germans. Instead there will be an understanding between the various language elements of the one good ruling race.

DAP Characteristics

Although the party was, according to its name, a party of the working class, most of the membership came from the middle class. Ordinary German workers, both in 1919 and up until the Nazis gained power in 1932, would remain loyal to the Communist Party and the liberal Social Democrats.

The men who made up the fledgling Nazi Party came for the most part from lower-middle-class families and were between twenty and thirty-five years old. Many were former soldiers who came home from the war without a profession. Of these, many were violent by nature and were attracted by the prospect of street brawling. Some were middle-class shopkeepers frightened by the thought of a Communist government. A few were upper-middle-class businessmen who saw in the DAP a way to recover from the economic catastrophe that had followed World War I.

Generally, the early Nazis were characterized by four qualities: a fierce love of Germany, a hatred of Jews, a fear of communism, and a distrust of the Weimar Republic. By 1923 many of what would be the heart of the Nazi Party—Ernst Röhm, Rudolph Hess, Alfred Rosenberg, Julius Streicher, and Hermann Göring—had already placed themselves at Hitler's side.

Röhm was a born fighter. "Since I am an immature and wicked man," he once said, "war and unrest appeal to me more than

Members of the Nazi Party parade with banners in 1923. Most of the early Nazis came from lower-middle-class families and were extremely patriotic.

good order."[25] Röhm reveled in violence and took delight in personally leading his men in street battles against the Communists. He heard Hitler speak in 1919 and thought he had found the savior of Germany. As deputy commander of the army division in Munich, he was in a position to help the DAP acquire both weapons and men. He recruited for the party many Free Corps members and former soldiers who later—led by Röhm himself—would carry out the Nazi doctrine of brutality against the Jews.

Hess, the son of a merchant, had been wounded twice during the war and afterwards abandoned his university studies to fight with the Free Corps and distribute anti-Jewish propaganda. While in college, Hess became a passionate German nationalist who predicted that a leader would arise who would lead the country to world dominance:

> He himself has nothing in common with the mass; like every great man he is all personality. . . . When necessity commands, he does not shrink before bloodshed. Great questions are always decided by blood and iron. . . . In order to reach his goal, he is prepared to trample on his closest friends. . . . The lawgiver proceeds with terrible hardness.[26]

Hess became Hitler's closest and most loyal friend and, for a time, deputy führer of the party.

Hitler's Cronies

Alfred Rosenberg, who later would play a major role in the extermination of Jews in eastern Europe, settled in Munich in 1920 and on meeting Hitler saw in him the person who would lead the Aryan race to victory. Rosenberg wrote several influential

Rudolf Hess was part of Hitler's inner political circle and one of his most trusted friends.

books, including *The Myth of the 20th Century*, in which he maintained that everything noble in the world was due to the efforts of the Aryans while everything inferior was the work of the Jews. Hitler was instantly attracted to Rosenberg, whose views helped shape and focus his own anti-Semitism.

Julius Streicher was perhaps the most unsavory character in the DAP. An elementary school teacher, he founded a right-wing party based solely on anti-Semitism. Streicher was a psychotic whose fantasies found outlets in bizarre sexual behavior and his loathing of the Jews. He was also fond of inflicting physical pain and seldom appeared in public without a whip in his hand. In 1921 Streicher fell under Hitler's spell and brought his entire party into the DAP camp. In 1923 he founded a newspaper, *Der Stürmer* (*The Stormer*) that in lurid, pornographic terms portrayed Jews as perverts, rapists of Aryan girls, and murderers and mutilators of Christian children. Such stories, published repeatedly over the years, helped convince millions of Germans that Jews had no place in their country or, indeed, on earth.

Göring was not typical of the early Nazis. The son of a well-to-do colonial official, he was one of Germany's foremost combat pilots during World War I and enjoyed tremendous popularity. In 1921 he decided to become a follower of Hitler. He rose rapidly and was eventually the number-two man in the Nazi Party and the man designated by Hitler as his successor. He was one of the rare Nazis who possessed wealth

Julius Streicher (front row, fourth from left) founded the anti-Semitic paper Der Stürmer. *The paper fueled the already rampant anti-Semitism of the German people and was a key propaganda instrument for the Nazi Party.*

and culture, and with his connections was able to introduce Hitler to many influential people. He was also an atypical Nazi in that he had no deep-seated hatred of Jews and no burning vision of German supremacy. Rather, Göring was a realist whose only aim was personal power.

Hitler Takes Charge

It was Hitler, however, who was the driving force behind the DAP from the moment he joined the party. Within a month he had overhauled party propaganda with grand plans. He began to organize a huge rally and rented an auditorium that seated nearly two thousand. His fellow members thought he had lost his mind. Harrer, the party chairman, resigned in protest.

The people of Munich, curious about this new party and its fiery spokesman, almost filled the hall. Hitler later called his speech of February 24, 1920, the point at which "the party burst the narrow bonds of a small club and for the first time exerted a determining influence on the mightiest factor of our time: public opinion."[27] He spoke for nearly four hours, outlining Germany's economic troubles and placing the blame on the "November criminals" and on the Jews. What should be done, he screamed, with those who had done this to Germany? "Hang them!"[28] the crowd screamed back.

Hitler then presented his party's twenty-five-point platform. Some planks, such as the elimination of interest and the sharing of business profits with the workers, had been concocted by Hitler to attract the masses and

Göring was an atypical Nazi both in class and attitude. Highly educated and with no particular hatred of the Jews, Göring nevertheless joined and furthered the cause of the Nazi Party.

would be quickly forgotten once the Nazis came to power. Some others, however, showed clearly the Nazi vision of the future. All Germans, the *Völk*, were to be united in a single nation. This nation would be entitled to *lebensraum*, "living space," for the German people. German citizenship was to be reserved for those of pure Aryan blood. "No Jew, therefore," Hitler said, "may be a member of the nation."[29]

A week later, the party officially changed its name to the *Nationalsozialistische Deutsche*

Arbeiterpartei—the National Socialist German Workers' Party—soon shortened to "Nazi." The new name was intended to convey the image of the party as socialist—and thus a party of the ordinary worker—but also nationalist, placing the destiny of Germany above any economic or class distinction.

The Nazis, in Hitler's view, would not be a traditional political party, electing candidates to public office. Rather, it would be a movement—something like a religion—that would sweep away all opposition. Such a movement, Hitler knew, must appeal to the emotions more than to the intellect. "Whoever wishes to win over the masses must know the key that will open the door to their hearts," he wrote. "It is not objectivity, which is a feckless [feeble] attitude, but a determined will, backed up by power if necessary."[30]

Nazi Symbolism

In creating Nazi symbolism, Hitler borrowed freely. In Vienna he had seen the effectiveness of the socialists' mass rallies.

The Power of the Spoken Word

Perhaps Adolf Hitler's greatest ability was the power to sway people, both individually and in groups, by the power of the spoken word. His fiery speeches, more than anything else, were responsible for the growth of the Nazi Party in its early years. One of Hitler's most bitter enemies inside the party, Otto Strasser, nevertheless admired and respected Hitler's talents as an orator. In his book *Hitler and I*, quoted in Allan Bullock's *Hitler: A Study in Tyranny*, Strasser analyzes this talent.

Hitler responds to the vibration of the human heart with the delicacy of a seismograph, or perhaps of a wireless receiving set, enabling him, with a certainty with which no conscious gift could endow him, to act as a loudspeaker proclaiming the most secret desires, the least admissible instincts, the sufferings, and personal revolts of a whole nation. . . . I have been asked many times what is the secret of Hitler's extraordinary power as a speaker. I can only attribute it to his uncanny intuition, which infallibly diagnoses the ills from which his audience is suffering. If he tries to bolster up his arguments with theories or quotations from books he has only imperfectly understood, he scarcely rises above a very poor mediocrity. But let him throw away his crutches and step out boldly, speaking as the spirit moves him, and he is promptly transformed into one of the greatest speakers of the century. . . . Adolf Hitler enters a hall. He sniffs the air. For a minute he gropes, feels his way, senses the atmosphere. Suddenly he bursts forth. His words go like an arrow to their target, he touches each private wound on the raw, liberating the mass unconscious, expressing its innermost aspirations, telling it what it most wants to hear.

"The broad masses of a population are more amenable to the appeal of rhetoric than to any other force,"[31] he wrote. He had witnessed the effect of thousands of people marching through the streets. Such rallies were meant to convey strength and power, and Hitler would plan each Nazi mass meeting in great detail.

Hitler knew that most people would be more easily unified by visible symbols than by abstract ideas. One was already at hand. The swastika—in German the *hakenkreuz*, or "crooked cross"—had been in use for thousands of years. It had been used as a symbol in ancient cultures and more recently by *völkisch* groups and by the members of the Free Corps.

Hitler also personally searched libraries for the correct version of the eagle that would appear atop the standards under which Nazi forces would parade. These standards, much like those carried by the legions of ancient Rome, featured the eagle atop a swastika underneath which was the local party shield with the Nazi slogan *Deutschland, Erwacht!*— "Germany, Awake!"

As early as 1920 the Nazi salute—the right arm held out stiffly at an angle—was in use, as was the greeting *heil*, variously translated as "saved" or "healed." Years later, when Hitler had become absolute leader of the Nazis, the greeting became "Heil, Hitler."

As much as he was convinced of the power of oratory and symbolism, Hitler knew that physical force played a large role in the politics of the time. It was routine for rival groups to send gangs of thugs to break up one another's meetings. In the summer of 1920 he organized a strong-arm squad to protect Nazi meetings and to disrupt those of the communists. The next year, the group, organized as a paramilitary unit, took the name *Sturmabteilung*, or Storm Detachment, and its members were known as storm troopers. In Germany it was known by its initials, SA.

The SA was the Nazis' private army, attracting former soldiers, Free Corps

A poster exhibits the symbols Hitler selected to define the Nazi Party—the eagle and the swastika. The slogan "Deutschland, erwacht!" is prominently displayed at the top.

members, bullies, and brawlers. Hitler did not care where his men came from or what they had been. "Such elements are unusable in times of peace," he said, "but in turbulent periods it's quite different."[32] By the fall of 1922, the SA had swelled to fifteen thousand men and Göring was made its commander.

Birth of the SS

Hitler eventually realized that the SA presented a potential problem. Many of its officers considered it the core of what would be a new German army. Hitler, on the other hand, saw that he needed a personal group of bodyguards loyal only to him. In 1923 he organized such a group, the *Stabswache* (Headquarters Guard), made up of some of the most trusted storm troopers. The *Stabswache* distinguished itself from the SA by wearing black ski caps with silver buttons in the shape of a skull. Later, the group would change its name to the *Schutzstaffel* (Protective Squad) and would terrorize Europe under its initials—the SS.

In the summer of 1921 Drexler and others among Hitler's colleagues grew jealous of his growing power. Taking advantage of Hitler's absence in Berlin, they approached some other right-wing groups about a merger, hoping an infusion of new members would dilute Hitler's importance. Hitler hurried back to Munich and took his opponents completely by surprise by resigning from the party.

His opponents knew that if Hitler left, the Nazi Party would lose much of its popular and monetary support. When Hitler said he would rejoin the party only on his terms, they pragmatically gave in. At a party congress on July 29, Hitler was given what amounted to dictatorial powers in complete accordance with his belief in the *führerprinzip*, or leadership principle. "There

must be no majority decisions," he wrote, "but only responsible persons. . . . Surely every man will have advisers by his side, but the decision will be made by one man. . . . Only he alone may possess the authority and the right to command."[33] *Der Führer*, or the leader, as he would henceforth be known, had arrived.

By the fall of 1923 the political situation in Germany had reached a low point. It took 4 billion German marks to buy one U.S. dollar, and thus the life savings of thousands of families, were now worthless. Hitler thought the time had come to seize control of the country.

The Nazi plan was first to take control of Bavaria and then to march the SA and army troops loyal to Bavaria to Berlin and overthrow the republic. The three most powerful men in the Bavarian government—Gustav Ritter von Kahr, General Otto von Lossow, and Colonel Hans von Seisser—discussed cooperating, but Hitler could not get their firm commitment. On November 7, Hitler and leaders of other right-wing groups met to plot a putsch, or armed revolt. The plan was to force Kahr, Lossow, and Seisser to join the revolt. They would all be given high offices in the new government, which would be headed by General Erich Ludendorff, a World War I hero and a leader of one of the right-wing groups.

The Beer Hall Putsch

The plotters chose to strike during a political meeting at the Bürgerbräukeller, a huge Munich beer hall. Kahr was scheduled to be the main speaker and Lossow and Seisser would be present, as would every major political figure in Munich.

At 8 P.M. on November 8, Kahr was in the midst of his speech when Göring burst

Hitler maneuvered his way to power while Germany's economic situation was at its worst. Here, poor men in Berlin await their chance to receive a bowl of soup.

through the doors followed by twenty-five storm troopers carrying pistols and machine guns. Hitler, who had been standing silently beside a pillar, leaped to the top of a table and fired a pistol shot into the air, crying, "The national revolution has broken out. . . . This hall is occupied by six hundred armed men, and no one may leave it."[34] He forced Kahr, Lossow, and Seisser into a side room where he told them that he had taken power and that they were to be members of the new government of Germany. Hitler was to be its head and Ludendorff would command the army.

Leaving the stunned trio, Hitler returned to the main hall and announced to the ner-

vous crowd that Kahr, Lossow, and Seisser had agreed to be part of the government and that General Ludendorff was on his way. Encouraged, the crowd began to cheer. When Ludendorff arrived, he was furious on learning that not he, but Hitler, was to lead the new government. Nevertheless, he reassured the crowd that all was well. Kahr, Lossow, and Seisser now made an appearance and vowed to support the new government.

Hitler then made a fatal mistake. He left to join some SA troops who were attempting to take over an army barracks. While he was gone, Kahr, Lossow, and Seisser talked Ludendorff into releasing them. Once free, the trio renounced their support and began to rally the troops and police loyal to them.

The next morning, a column of three thousand Nazis marched toward Munich's central plaza. Arm-in-arm in the front row were Ludendorff, Göring, Hitler, and Max von Scheubner-Richter. At the Odeonplatz they found their way barred by a hundred police armed with rifles. The Nazis advanced, bayonets fixed to their rifles.

As the two forces were about to come together, a shot rang out—no one could tell from which side. In an instant there were volleys of gunfire from both directions. Göring fell, shot in the thigh. Scheubner-Richter was fatally wounded and, in falling, dragged Hitler to the pavement and separated his shoulder. Nineteen Nazis were killed and dozens wounded. The rest scrambled for safety, including Hitler, who was rushed away in a party car. Only Ludendorff continued to march forward and was arrested on the spot.

The so-called Beer Hall Putsch had failed. Two days later Hitler was arrested. Göring and Hess fled to Austria. Röhm and the rest of the top Nazis were rounded up and arrested. The party was declared banned by the government. To all appearances, the Nazi Party and the career of Adolf Hitler were at an end. In fact, they had barely begun.

Years of Growth

Early in 1924, the Nazi Party seemed doomed. Its bid for power had failed. Its leaders either were under arrest or had fled the country. Spurred by the unyielding will of Adolf Hitler, however, the Nazis slowly rebuilt—gaining converts, molding a sophisticated organization, working within the political system, and waiting for the day when events would give them another opportunity to control Germany.

Hitler was so devastated by the failure of the Beer Hall Putsch that he attempted suicide. He was in the act of turning a revolver on himself when the wife of one of his followers wrestled it from his hand. Taken after his arrest to Landsberg prison about fifty miles west of Munich, he expected to be shot immediately. Instead, he was charged with high treason; with renewed hope, he resolved to use his trial as a stage from which to proclaim his Nazi philosophy.

The trial began on February 24, 1924. There were nine other defendants, including the famous General Ludendorff, but Hitler dominated the proceedings from the start. The trial was front-page news throughout Germany, and several foreign correspondents in attendance gave Hitler his first international exposure.

Given broad leeway to address the court by the sympathetic chief judge, Hitler freely admitted what he and the Nazis had done but argued that it was impossible for any patriotic German to commit treason against the "November criminals." He lashed out at his accusers—Kahr, Lossow, and Seisser— saying "they shared the same goal with us; namely the removal of the Reich [republic] government."[35] He acknowledged that he wanted to become a dictator. "The man who feels called upon to govern a people has no right to say, 'If you want me or summon me, I will co-operate.' No! It is his duty to step forward."[36] Finally, he told the court:

> Gentlemen, judgment will not be passed on us by you; judgment will be passed on us by the eternal court of history. . . . This other court, however, will not ask: "Did you or did you not commit high treason?" That court will pass judgment on us . . . who as Germans wanted the best for their people and their country, who were willing to fight and die for it.[37]

Vindication Through Guilt

The court found Hitler guilty and sentenced him to the lightest possible punishment, five years in prison with eligibility for parole in six months. The other defendants also received light sentences, and Ludendorff was acquitted altogether. The chief

After being charged with treason in 1924, Hitler (second from left) and co-conspirators await the court's verdict. Hitler was found guilty, but sentencing was light—five years in prison with a possibility of parole in six months.

judge commented on the "pure patriotic motives and honorable intentions"[38] of the men on trial, and the courtroom rang with cheers and cries of "Bravo!" as Hitler was taken to prison.

Prison was anything but harsh for Hitler and his fellow Nazis. They occupied spacious, sunny rooms decorated with swastika banners. There was plenty of good food, and the guards were friendly. Nazi sympa-

thizers showered them with gifts. One later said that Hitler's cell "looked like a delicatessen store. You could have opened up a flower and fruit and a wine shop with all the stuff stacked there."[39]

Hitler decided to use his time to write a book that would set forth for the whole world what the Nazi Party believed, what its goals were, and how those goals were to be achieved. Hitler wanted to title his book

Four and a Half Years of Struggle Against Lies, Stupidity, and Cowardice. His publisher, however, considered this far too long and convinced the author to shorten the title to *Mein Kampf* (*My Struggle*).

Mein Kampf would become the bible of the Nazis. Despite its great length, ponderous style, and endless repetition of the same basic themes, it became one of the world's best-known books. By the end of World War II in 1945, more than 10 million copies in sixteen languages had been sold. Hitler's share of the sales of *Mein Kampf* would provide the bulk of his income for the rest of his life.

Those who hoped to find in *Mein Kampf* the inside story of the Beer Hall Putsch or intimate details of Hitler's life were disappointed. Hitler glosses over his childhood and his years in Vienna, suppressing some facts and inventing others. Instead, *Mein Kampf* revolves around four themes: the supreme importance of race, the survival of the fittest, the need for a militaristic state with a dictator at its head, and the destiny of Germany to be the dominant world power.

The subsequent actions of Hitler and the Nazis should have surprised neither Germany nor the rest of the world. The plan is there for all to read. All races, he writes, are constituted of superior or inferior blood, and the highest blood is that of the Germans. Germans, therefore, are the culture creators, the master race, and have a right to *lebensraum* at the expense of inferior races, specifically the people to the east in Poland and the Soviet Union. These people are destined to serve the Germans under the light of German culture.

The Role of the Jews

As for the Jews, they are incapable of being enlightened by German culture. Instead, they are destroyers of culture, defilers of Aryan blood, the enemies of all that is noble and pure. Throughout the pages of *Mein Kampf*, Hitler heaps abuse on the Jews, calling them

Hitler used his time in prison to write Mein Kampf—*a rambling, self-congratulatory account of the development of his anti-Semitic beliefs. By the end of the war, the controversial book had sold over 10 million copies and had been printed in sixteen languages.*

Mein Kampf

Adolf Hitler's book *Mein Kampf* (*My Struggle*) was the bible of Nazi Germany. Written while Hitler was imprisoned in 1924 after the failure of the Beer Hall Putsch, the book sets forth Hitler's entire philosophy—his belief in the destiny of Germany, his hatred of the Jews and other "subhuman" races—as well as his plans for conquering lands to the east. In his biography of Hitler, Robert Payne gave this evaluation of *Mein Kampf*. It is quoted in Yehuda Bauer's *A History of the Holocaust*.

It is a great book in the sense that Machiavelli's *The Prince* is a great book, casting a long shadow. The Renaissance word *terribilita* implies a superb daring, immense disdain, an absolute lack of scruples [ethics], and a terrifying determination to ride roughshod over all obstacles, and the book possesses all these qualities. The author says, "This is the kind of man I am, and this is what I shall do." and he conceals nothing, as though too disdainful of his enemies to wear a disguise. The armed bohemian describes in minute detail how he will stalk his prey. . . . There is no evidence that [Stanley] Baldwin, [Neville] Chamberlain, [Winston] Churchill, [Franklin] Roosevelt, [Joseph] Stalin, or any of the political leaders most directly affected did anything more than glance at it. If they had read it with the attention it deserves, they would have seen that it was a blueprint for the total destruction of bourgeois [upper-middle-class] society and the conquest of the world. . . . The ideas he expresses—hatred for the Jews, the insignificance of men, the necessity of a Führer figure possessing supreme authority, the purity of the German race so immeasurably superior to all other races, the need for living space in the East, his absolute detestation of Bolshevism [communism]—all these are announced with manic force.

"maggots," "blood-suckers," "vampires," "a pestilence," and "personifications of the Devil." The goal of the Jews, he writes, is to defile the German race, dilute the pure Aryan blood, and take control of the world.

What does Hitler say should be done with the Jews? *Mein Kampf* is not specific except in saying they will have no place whatsoever in the greater Germany. One passage, however, grimly foreshadows the Holocaust:

If, at the beginning of the War [World War I] and during the War, twelve or fifteen thousand of these Hebraic corrupters of the nation had been subjected to poison gas such as had to be endured in the field by hundreds of thousands of our very best German workers . . . then the sacrifice of millions at the front would not have been in vain. On the contrary: twelve thousand scoundrels opportunely eliminated and perhaps a million orderly, worth-while Germans had been saved for the future.[40]

While Hitler wrote, the Nazis on the outside were in disarray. Hitler had appointed Alfred Rosenberg to lead the party in his absence, perhaps because he knew that Rosenberg was not strong enough to hold it together and therefore would pose no threat to him. Although the party was officially banned, two rival factions sprang up, one led by Ludendorff and Röhm (out of prison on parole) and the other by Streicher and Herman Esser. Ludendorff's group combined with other right-wing groups to form the Völkisch Social Bloc to field a slate of candidates in state and national elections.

The Beer Hall Putsch had taught Hitler that the best way to gain power was through the electoral system rather than armed rebellion. But Hitler also had seen that any coalition would weaken the Nazis, and he objected to the party's taking part in the spring elections. Rosenberg, however, sided with Ludendorff; ultimately the Völkisch Social Bloc finished a strong third in the state election and sent thirty-two members to the Reichstag, including Röhm and Ludendorff, the first Nazis elected to public office.

A Hitler Surprise

Hitler, meanwhile, tired of trying to keep the peace between the various Nazi elements, surprised everyone by issuing a statement that he was withdrawing completely from politics "until my restored freedom offers me the possibility of being a real leader."[41] In this way, he could both avoid taking sides and ensure that the party would delay any move to unite until he was freed. Finally, he realized that his active political involvement from inside prison might jeopardize his chances for parole.

The success of the Nazis and other right-wing groups at the ballot box was short-lived. When national elections were held in December 1924, the *völkisch* parties lost most of their seats in the Reichstag. In Bavaria, the right-wing vote fell to 5 percent from 16 percent the previous spring. Given the poor showing in the election, the Bavarian government decided Hitler was no longer a threat and granted his parole. On December 20 he was released and returned to Munich.

Both the parties of the extreme right and the extreme left (the Communists) had lost ground in the December election, primarily because Germany was finally recovering from World War I. The monetary crisis had eased. Reparation payments had been reduced and the way opened

Alfred Rosenberg, in charge of the Nazi Party during Hitler's imprisonment, could not keep the group from splintering into several factions.

for international loans, other countries having decided that a strong German economy was to everyone's benefit.

Relations with other countries improved. In 1926 Germany joined the League of Nations, an international body formed after World War I, and signed several treaties in which nations of the world pledged to renounce war as a method of resolving disputes. The standing of the Weimar Republic received a boost, both outside and inside Germany, when the respected General Hindenburg won the presidency. Times were better in Germany. The voices of the Nazis, always most persuasive to the discontented, fell on deaf ears.

And yet, all was not as stable as it seemed. The Weimar Republic still enjoyed only lukewarm support. Of the ten major political parties, only two were committed to the republic. Many of the strongest segments of German society—industry, the legal profession, the universities, and especially the military—remained distrustful of democracy. And, uncomfortable with the increasingly liberated lifestyles of the so-called Roaring Twenties, the vast majority of Germans were inclined to return to the old, conservative ways.

Hitler's Mission

Once released from prison Hitler's mission was to rebuild the Nazi Party into an organization that would take power legally,

Hitler leaves Landsberg prison in 1924 to once again resume leadership of the Nazi Party. Hitler immediately made several inflammatory speeches that caused officials to ban him from public speaking.

appealing to the broad mass of German voters. "Instead of working to achieve power by [force], we shall have to hold our noses and enter the Reichstag against the Catholic and Marxist deputies," he said. "If out-voting them takes longer than out-shooting them, at least the result will be guaranteed by their own Constitution."[42] His first step in this new strategy was to restore the party to legal status. He personally convinced Bavarian officials to lift the ban on the Nazis and to permit the Nazi newspaper, the *Völkischer*

Beobachter, to resume publication.

The ban was lifted, and nearly four thousand Nazis met in the Bürgerbräukeller, site of the abortive Beer Hall Putsch, to celebrate. In front of a cheering crowd, Hitler sounded anything but law-abiding: "To this struggle of ours there are only two possible issues: either the enemy passes over our bodies or we pass over theirs."[43] Understandably nervous Bavarian officials promptly banned him from public speaking; most other German states followed suit.

Hitler's Challenge

When Adolf Hitler was released from prison late in 1924, the Nazi Party organization was in a shambles. Those in northern Germany were attacking the Catholic Church, which was very strong in the Nazis' home base of Bavaria. Party members had, against Hitler's wishes, participated in elections. Ernst Röhm, whose vision of the SA differed from Hitler's, had resigned and left Germany.

Hitler needed to show that he was still in command. He chose to do so in a speech on February 27, 1925. He spoke in the Bürgerbräukeller, the same beer hall in which his abortive revolt had taken place. He had promised the state officials of Bavaria that he would be moderate in his speeches, but, as quoted in Allan Bullock's *Hitler: A Study in Tyranny*, the end of his two-hour speech was anything but restrained:

If anyone comes and wants to impose conditions on me, I shall say to him:

"Just wait, my young friend, and see what conditions I impose on you." I am not contending for the favour of the masses. At the end of a year you shall judge, my comrades. If I have acted rightly, well and good. If I have acted wrongly, I shall resign my office into your hands. Until then, however, I alone lead the movement, and no one can impose conditions on me so long as I personally bear the responsibility. And I once more bear the whole responsibility for everything that occurs in the movement. . . . To this struggle of ours there are only two possible issues: either the enemy pass over our bodies or we pass over theirs, and it is my desire that, if in the struggle I should fall, the Swastika banner shall be my winding sheet.

This was too much for the officials of Bavaria. Hitler was forbidden to speak in public and threatened with reimprisonment if he ignored the ban.

Undaunted, Hitler began working behind the scenes. Between 1925 and 1927 the Nazi Party would be reorganized from top to bottom and anyone not absolutely loyal to Hitler and his goals would be shoved aside. One of the first to go was Ludendorff. The general had outlived his usefulness to the Nazis, and his increasing attacks on Catholicism were hurting the party in strongly Catholic Bavaria. After several bitter arguments with Hitler, Ludendorff quit the party.

Röhm too was a thorn in Hitler's side. While Hitler was in prison, Röhm had built up a new political organization, the *Frontbann*, that took in members of other rightwing groups. He had not given up on the idea of an armed takeover, and even envisioned the SA as a replacement of the regular German army rather than as an arm of the Nazis. In April 1925, Hitler confronted Röhm and ordered him to toe the line or resign. Röhm chose to resign and four years later left Germany.

Strasser's Challenge

The most serious challenge to Hitler's authority came from a group headed by Gregor Strasser. Strasser had become a Nazi in 1920 and was district leader in lower Bavaria. Fiercely independent, he refused to acknowledge Hitler as absolute leader. He had worked closely with Ludendorff in creating the Völkisch Social Bloc and was one of the Nazis elected to the Reichstag in 1924.

Hitler distrusted Strasser but needed his abilities, especially his good political contacts in northern Germany, where the Nazis were weakest. Assigned by Hitler to strengthen the party there, within a few months Strasser had built up a formidable organization throughout the north and west. To Hitler's dismay, however, Strasser

Lebensraum

When Hitler was building the Nazi Party in the 1920s, he preached that the destiny of Germany was to find what he called *lebensraum*, or "living space," in the areas to the east, namely Czechoslovakia, Poland, and the Soviet Union. These excerpts from *Mein Kampf*, quoted in William Shirer's *The Rise and Fall of the Third Reich*, make it abundantly clear what path Hitler would follow if the Nazis ever gained power.

[German expansion] was possible only in the East. . . . If land was desired in Europe, it could be obtained by and large only at the expense of Russia, and this meant that the new Reich must again set itself on the march along the road of the Teutonic Knights of old, to obtain by the German sword sod for the German plow and daily bread for the nation. . . . Only an adequate large space on this earth assures a nation of freedom of existence. . . . Without consideration of "traditions" and prejudices [the Nazis] must find the courage to gather our people from its present restricted living space to new land and soil. . . . The National Socialist movement must strive to eliminate the disproportion between our population and our area—viewing this latter as a source of food as well as a basis for power politics. . . . We must hold unflinchingly to our aim . . . to secure for the German people the land and soil to which they are entitled.

Gregor Strasser opposed many of Hitler's policy platforms, including his animosity toward the Communists and the Socialists.

took seriously the "socialism" in National Socialism. He wanted to nationalize major industries, and even went so far as to propose a working relationship with the Communist Party.

Matters came to a head when Strasser proposed that the Nazis support Communist-proposed legislation enabling the state to take over the fortunes of the former nobility. Hitler, who at the time was seeking upper-class support, was furious. In January 1926, without Hitler's permission, Strasser called a meeting of Nazi leaders in the northern city of Hanover. Hitler did not attend. At the meeting, Strasser and several of his supporters called for an end to Hitler's absolute leadership, pointing out correctly that he was not even a German citizen.

Finally, however, they agreed that the party needed Hitler.

Hitler struck back the next month, calling another meeting, this time in the southern city of Bamberg, where the northern leaders were outnumbered by Hitler's supporters. Speaking for four hours, Hitler forcefully told the group that there would be no deviation from the party's opposition to socialism and communism and that he was to be obeyed as ultimate leader of the party. Most of the northern leaders came over to Hitler's side, and the rest were too divided among themselves to mount a challenge, especially after Strasser was injured in an automobile accident shortly afterward.

Joseph Goebbels

Hitler's key convert among the dissident group was Strasser's secretary, Joseph Goebbels. A handsome, highly intelligent man who walked with a limp because of a deformed foot, Goebbels had earned a doctoral degree in literature but failed as a poet, playwright, and journalist. Embittered, he blamed Jewish publishers and drifted into the Nazi Party. He was attracted by Strasser's brand of "Germany first" socialism and edited Strasser's party newsletter. He was a strong supporter of Strasser in his quarrel with Hitler and at the January 1926 meeting even called for Hitler to be expelled from the party.

Hitler, however, saw Goebbels's ability and made a concerted effort to win his loyalty. He invited Goebbels to Munich and allowed him to be the principal speaker at a Nazi rally. Later in 1926 Hitler made Goebbels coleader of the Berlin Nazi Party. Goebbels was completely won over and remained Hitler's most loyal aide. He was a masterful speaker, almost as spellbinding as Hitler, and a brilliant manipulator of public opinion. It was Goebbels who was to build the propaganda machinery that would eventually make Hitler a virtual god in the eyes of the German people.

By the end of 1926, Hitler had reestablished himself as the unchallenged leader of the Nazis. He then turned his efforts to building up the party, not only in terms of numbers of dues-paying members, but also as a movement. His two goals were to achieve highly efficient military-style organization and at the same time reach out to all segments of German society. Nazism was to be more than a political party; it was to be a way of life.

The political organization of the Nazis was borrowed from the Soviet Communist Party. The country was divided into thirty-six districts, or *Gaue*, each headed by a *Gauleiter* answerable only to Hitler. The *Gaue* were further divided into *Kreise*, or circles, then into *Ortsgruppen*, or local groups. In cities, there were even smaller neighborhood cells headed by a *Blockwart*, or block warden. Reporting directly to Hitler, who carried the official title of führer, were several *Reichleiter*, or state leaders, who oversaw various departments. Also reporting directly to Hitler were the military arms of the party, the SA and the SS.

Germany Nazified

At the same time the Nazis were streamlining their organization, they were bringing more groups of people under the party umbrella. Hitler's idea was to create a parallel society, with Nazism permeating every aspect of German life. For young boys and girls, a *Jugendbund*, or youth association, was formed, later to be known as the Hitler Youth. Other organizations catered to college students, pupils in elementary school, teachers, and housewives. The Nazis also reached into the professions, sponsoring associations of doctors, lawyers, civil servants, and artists.

A photo of Joseph Goebbels reveals his right club foot. A convincing speaker, Goebbels was wooed away from Gregor Strasser by Hitler, who immediately saw his talents.

The Wooing of Goebbels

Adolf Hitler was just as persuasive in a one-on-one situation as he was in front of a crowd. A good example of this ability was his courtship of Joseph Goebbels, who, as secretary to Gregor Strasser, had been a Hitler opponent and at one point called for his expulsion from the Nazi Party.

Hitler, however, recognized Goebbels's talents and set about to win his loyalty. The stages of his conversion are shown in the diary he kept, these passages from which are found in William Shirer's *The Rise and Fall of the Third Reich*.

First, on February 15, 1926, Goebbels wrote:

> Hitler talks for two hours. I feel as though someone had beaten me. What sort of Hitler is this? A reactionary? Extremely awkward and unsteady. Completely wrong on the Russian question. Italy and England are our natural allies! Horrible! . . . We must annihilate Russia! . . . The question of the private property to the nobility must not even be touched upon. Terrible! . . . Certainly one of the great disappointments of my life. I no longer have complete faith in Hitler.

But then, on April 8, after a special invitation from Hitler to speak at Munich, he wrote, "I enter the hall. Roaring welcome. . . . And then I speak for two and a half hours. . . . People roar and shout. At the end Hitler embraces me. I feel happy. . . . Hitler is always at my side."

By August, Goebbels had surrendered completely. In an article in the Nazi newspaper, he addressed Strasser's group:

> Only now do I recognize you for what you are: revolutionaries in speech but not in deed. . . . We . . . bow to him . . . with the manly, unbroken pride of the ancient Norsemen who stand upright before their Germanic feudal lord. We feel that he is greater than all of us, greater than you and I. He is the instrument of the Divine Will that shapes history with fresh, creative passion.

Goebbels delivers a speech urging Germans to boycott Jewish-owned businesses.

Members of the Hitler Youth in Berlin ride in a truck that carries the slogan "The führer orders, we follow! All say yes!"

Steadily the Nazis became more visible throughout Germany. SA troops, now uniformed in brown shirts, marched through city streets in torchlight parades. In 1927 the Nazis staged the first of several party congresses in Nuremberg. Under the direction of Goebbels and Nazi architect Albert Speer, these mass meetings would evolve into gigantic ritual spectacles over which Hitler presided like a king.

And yet, with Germany sharing in general world prosperity, the growth of the Nazi Party was slow. By the end of 1925 there were only 27,000 members. This number rose to 49,000 in 1926, 72,000 in 1927, and 108,000 in 1928.

Those who joined the Nazi Party between 1925 and 1929 tended to be younger than members of rival parties. Two-thirds were between the ages of twenty and forty, perhaps lured by the party's reputation for activism or by Hitler's personal charisma.

The Nazis remained a party of the middle class. Though far outnumbered in the general population, almost as many white-collar workers joined as did ordinary wage earners. More than 18 percent of the Nazis were self-employed—shopkeepers, businessmen, professionals, and skilled craftsmen—

even though this group constituted only about 10 percent of the total German population.

Those who joined before 1929 formed the core of the party. They were the Nazis most loyal to Hitler and most in tune with his political, social, and racial views. From their ranks would come the leaders of Nazi Germany—Nazi officials, government workers, officers in the SA and SS. Although many would become directly involved in the Holocaust and commit the vilest atrocities, they were far from subhuman beasts on the surface. For the most part they were perfectly ordinary people, husbands and wives with families, jobs, social lives.

Despite their growth, the Nazis could make no headway at the polls. In the national elections of 1928, the party drew only 810,000 votes compared to almost 2 million in 1924.

Nevertheless, Hitler had laid the foundations for success. The Nazis, given up for lost after the failure of the Beer Hall Putsch in 1923, were by 1929 a highly organized, highly visible force in Germany. All they needed was an opportunity, and this would not be long in coming.

CHAPTER

4

The Seizure of Power

As the 1920s drew to a close, Adolf Hitler's Nazis had become a cohesive political force that was spreading its tentacles throughout Germany. Yet it remained one of the smaller of many parties on the political landscape. Before long, the Nazis would be propelled from obscurity, and the way would be opened for the Weimar Republic to be destroyed by the bickering and blunders of its leaders.

In mid-1929, Hitler was not widely known outside Bavaria. That status would change because of the Young Plan, named for the American banker who devised it. Under the plan Germany was obligated to pay World War I debts of 2 billion marks a year for thirty-seven years. Although these terms were more lenient than those originally imposed by the Versailles treaty, the right-wing parties were furious at what they considered a betrayal of Germany by the Weimar Republic. Led by Alfred Hugenberg of the National People's Party, they collected enough signatures to force a national referendum on the plan.

Hitler became lead spokesman for the group, and thanks to the newspapers and newsreel companies owned by Hugenberg, soon his face and words were seen and heard throughout the country. In August, the Nuremberg party rally drew more than 100,000. More than 30,000 storm troopers marched through the streets, among them the black-shirted SS under its new leader, Heinrich Himmler.

Himmler, a Bavarian who earned a degree in agriculture after serving in World War I, joined the Nazis in 1923 and played a minor role in the Beer Hall Putsch. He

Hitler gives the Nazi salute to thousands of supporters. Several economic and political factors would compel the party's quick ascension and complete control of the German government.

Hitler in Love

Adolf Hitler considered himself singled out by fate to lead Germany to greatness. As a result, he denied himself what he felt were ordinary, worldly pleasures, claiming that he belonged to the nation. He neither drank nor smoked. For most of his life he was a vegetarian.

He admired beautiful women but as a young man was too shy and too ashamed of his poverty to have anything to do with them. Late in his career he had a mistress, Eva Braun, whom he married only hours before his suicide in 1945. He enjoyed her company, but those who knew the pair never detected any great depth of emotion on Hitler's part.

The only woman Hitler truly loved was his niece, Geli Raubal, the daughter of his half-sister Angela. In 1925 Angela came to Munich to act as housekeeper for Hitler. With her came her daughters, Geli and Friedl. For the next six years, Geli, a bright, attractive seventeen-year-old, became the constant companion of the uncle who was her senior by twenty years. He took her to meetings, to concerts, to restaurants, and on long walks in the mountains.

The young woman was flattered by all the attention paid to her by Hitler, who at the time was becoming a well-known public figure. When she began to widen her circle of friends, however, Hitler became jealous and possessive. He refused to allow her any social life separate from his.

Geli grew increasingly frustrated over her lack of freedom. Finally, in September of 1931, they quarreled over Geli's proposed trip to Vienna. As Hitler was getting into his car, witnesses heard Geli shout to him from a window, "Then you won't let me go to Vienna?" Hitler shouted back, "No!"

The next morning, Geli Raubal was found shot to death in her room. Hitler was overcome with grief. Friends said he seriously thought of committing suicide. For the rest of his life he never spoke of Geli without tears in his eyes. Her room remained untouched. Her portrait was one of the few in Hitler's underground living quarters on the day he died.

Geli Raubal, Hitler's niece and true love. Hitler was grief stricken when the young woman was found dead of a gunshot wound.

served as Gregor Strasser's secretary and became *Gauleiter* of lower Bavaria when Strasser went to Berlin. Early in 1928 he became a poultry farmer but abandoned farming when Hitler named him to head the SS the next year. A mild-looking and apparently emotionless man, Himmler was nevertheless a fanatical racist. Under his leadership, the SS would eventually grow almost as large as the German army itself and would be the primary force by which the Nazis carried out the Holocaust.

The referendum against the Young Plan failed, but it was a victory for Hitler, whose ideas were made known to millions who had never heard of him before. Just as important, Hitler was introduced through Hugenberg to some of Germany's most powerful industrialists, some of whom would later supply the Nazis with funds.

Economic Depression

The second key event of 1929 for the Nazis was the crash of the stock market in the United States. The prosperity the Weimar Republic had enjoyed since 1924 was based on investments and loans from foreign countries, mainly America. When the flow of foreign funds stopped, the German economy collapsed. Businesses and banks failed; unemployment would rise from 3 million in 1929 to 6 million in 1932.

The situation was perfect for the Nazis and for Hitler, who wrote, "Never in my life have I been so well disposed and inwardly contented as in these days. For hard reality has opened the eyes of millions of Germans."[44] The Nazis immediately began taking their message to the people of Germany, blaming the country's troubles on the "November criminals" and claiming the economic depression was part of a worldwide Jewish conspiracy.

The Nazis were not the only ones trying to topple the republic. The army was concerned that the government might be too weak to prevent a Communist takeover. Army generals who were previously politically neutral (at least publicly) now took a more active role that eventually played into the hands of the Nazis. The chief plotter was General Kurt von Schleicher, who had great influence with President Hindenburg as a result of his friendship with Hindenburg's son Oskar, and who had been appointed chief liaison to the government by the minister of defense, General Wilhelm Groener.

Kurt von Schleicher was afraid that Hindenburg's weak control of the government might lead to a Communist takeover.

Schleicher convinced Hindenburg to withdraw his support from Chancellor Hermann Müller. When Müller resigned in March 1930, Schleicher proposed he appoint Heinrich Brüning, a member of the Catholic Center Party, a supporter of the military, and a strong opponent of the Versailles treaty, which limited the size of the army to 100,000 men. Brüning proposed to deal with the growing economic depression through a combination of higher taxes and budget cuts. His plan was attacked by both

Horst Wessel

The official song of the Nazi Party, and later the unofficial national anthem of Germany, was known as the Horst Wessel Song. Wessel was a young SA storm trooper who had dropped out of law school and defied his mother by joining the Nazis. He lived in a Berlin slum with a former prostitute. In January 1930, the woman's former boyfriend, a Communist, broke into Wessel's apartment and mortally wounded him.

Joseph Goebbels, the Nazis' propaganda chief, set out to make Wessel a martyr in the party's struggle with their Communist opponents. Wessel was given an elaborate funeral, which was interrupted by stone-throwing Communists. Goebbels turned even this to his advantage, later writing, "As the coffin came to rest in the cool ground there went up outside the gates the depraved cry of the subhuman. . . . The departed, still with us, raised his weary hand and beckoned into the shimmering distance: Forward over the graves! At the end of the road lies Germany."

A poem Wessel had written was put to music and became the marching song of the SA. This translation by Louis Snyder is found in his book *Encyclopedia of the Third Reich*.

Hold high the banner! Close the hard ranks serried! [crowded]

SA marches on with sturdy stride.

Comrades, by Red Front and Reaction killed, are buried,

But march with us in image at our side.

Gangway! Gangway! now for the Brown battalions!

For Storm Troopers clear roads o'er land!

The Swastika gives hope to our entranced millions,

The day for freedom and for bread's at hand.

The trumpet blows its shrill and final blast!

Prepared for war and battle here we stand.

Soon Hitler's banners will wave unchecked at last,

The end of German slav'ry in our land.

the Communists on the left and the National People's Party and the Nazis on the right, who jointly nicknamed Brüning the "hunger chancellor."

Rule by Decree

Realizing he could not get a majority in the Reichstag, Brüning appealed to Hindenburg to invoke Article 48 of the Weimar Constitution giving the chancellor authority to rule by executive decree without the consent of the legislature. When Hindenburg invoked Article 48, dissolved the Reichstag, and called for new elections, he had unwittingly started the process that would destroy democracy in Germany. From this point on, the Reichstag's potential to control or check Nazi power declined.

The Nazis saw the new elections as an opportunity to increase their representation in the Reichstag and threw themselves wholeheartedly into the campaign. First, however, Hitler had to deal with a mutiny within the SA, into which many unemployed workers had flocked. These new storm troopers were moved more by money than by political ideology and threatened public riots if their pay was not increased. Knowing that SA mob actions would hurt the Nazis' image in the upcoming elections, Hitler took personal command and, by the force of his personality, calmed his troops. Shortly afterward, he called on his old comrade Ernst Röhm, to return to Germany and take command of the SA.

The results of the September 14, 1930, elections surprised even the Nazis. Votes for Nazis rose from 810,000 in 1928 to 6.4 million—18 percent of the total. They placed 107 members in the 577-seat Reichstag and became the legislature's second-largest party. The election was a victory for extremism, since on the far left the Communists had

also increased their representation. As a result, the parties in the center were weakened, making it impossible for Brüning to get a working majority and forcing him to rule by decree.

Hitler's message was becoming increasingly popular throughout Germany as the country's economic troubles deepened. Between 1929 and 1933, party membership would leap from 129,000 to 850,000. More than ever, it was a party of youth. More than 40 percent of those who joined during the four-year period were between twenty-one and thirty years of age and almost 15,000 were in their late teens.

The Nazis had more success between 1929 and 1933 with ordinary workers than at any other time in their history. Most workers remained true to the Communists and Social Democrats, but about 200,000 cast their lot with the Nazis. In 1933 blue-collar workers made up 32.5 percent of the party—an all-time high.

As the months went by, opposition to Brüning grew. At the same time, Hitler began to increase his efforts to win support from both industry and the military. He told the businessmen, according to future Nazi minister of economics Walther Funk, "that he was an enemy of state economy and of so-called 'planned economy' and that he considered free enterprise and competition as absolutely necessary in order to gain the highest possible production."[45] So much for any notions of socialism.

Reassuring the Army

Hitler reassured the army that he was not out to replace the military establishment with the SA. He said publicly, "I have always held the view that any attempt to replace the Army was madness. None of us have any interest in replacing the Army. . . . We will see to it, when we have come to power, that out of the present Reichswehr [state army] a great Army of the German people shall rise."[46] Furthermore, he said, his idea of revolution meant "exclusively the rescue of the enslaved [by the Versailles treaty] German nation we have today."[47] This was what the generals wanted to hear, and they began to warm to both Hitler and the Nazis.

On October 10, 1931, Hitler had his first interview with Hindenburg, during which he delivered a long, impassioned speech on the evils of the republic. The old warrior was not impressed: "This Bohemian corporal wants to be Reich chancellor? Never! At most he could

Hindenburg tried to keep government control away from Hitler by running for the presidency at age eighty-four. Unfortunately, Hitler was able to gain a significant portion of the popular vote— enough to be a future contender for the chancellorship.

be my Postmaster General. Then he can lick me on the stamps from behind."[48]

Convinced by Brüning that Hitler was a threat, the eighty-four-year-old Hindenburg reluctantly agreed on February 15, 1932, to run for reelection to another seven-year term. While Hitler's chief followers waited impatiently, Hitler seesawed, trying to decide whether or not to challenge Hindenburg. At last, on February 22, he had Goebbels announce his intention to run for the presidency.

Before running for the presidency of Germany, however, Hitler had to become a German citizen. For almost ten years he had been a stateless person, Austria having revoked his citizenship. The problem was solved on February 25 when the Nazi minister of the interior of the state of Brunswick named Hitler a member of the official Brunswick delegation in Berlin. This officially made Hitler a German, three days after he had announced his candidacy for president.

The Nazis launched an all-out campaign. Hitler alone made 209 speeches. A special film was distributed to theaters and a special magazine published. Storm troopers staged torchlight parades in cities throughout the country. Hitler lost with 30.2 percent of the vote, but Hindenburg's 49.7 percent was just short of the majority needed to avoid a runoff. In the runoff, Hindenburg won again, but Hitler picked up an additional 2 million votes.

Hitler's success made Brüning even more nervous. Three days after the runoff election, the government, at the urging of Brüning and General Groener, outlawed the SA, SS, and Hitler Youth. The ban actually worked to the advantage of the Nazis, however, because the army, now increasingly on Hitler's side, opposed the move. When

An election poster attempts to appeal to the working-class voter with the words "Workers elect the frontline soldier, Hitler!"

Groener rose in the Reichstag to defend his action, he was shouted down by the Nazis, led by Hermann Göring, who had returned to Germany and was once again one of Hitler's top lieutenants. Groener did such a poor job of replying, becoming confused and stumbling over his words, that Schleicher coldly informed him he had lost the confidence of the army and must resign, which he did three days later.

The Fall of Brüning

Brüning was next to fall. Schleicher realized that the chancellor had fallen out of favor with Hindenburg, who blamed him for Hitler's strong showing in the presidential election. He convinced Hindenburg to dismiss Brüning. Brüning's successor was an obscure, middle-of-the-road politician named Franz von Papen. Papen had the backing of Schleicher, who thought he could be controlled, and of Hitler, because he promised to lift the ban on the SA and SS.

Four days after becoming chancellor, Papen dissolved the Reichstag and scheduled new elections. Two weeks later, he lifted the ban on the SA. The storm troopers celebrated by marching through the streets, singing,

> Blood must flow, blood must flow!
>
> Blood must flow as cudgel [club] thick as hail!
>
> Let's smash it up, Let's smash it up
>
> That God-damned Jewish republic.[49]

National elections were conducted on July 31. The Nazis received 13.7 million votes, won 230 seats in the Reichstag—of which Göring was elected president—and replaced the Social Democrats as the largest party. From his new position of power, Hitler cast his eye on the chancellor's palace. In August he told Hindenburg that he would join the new government, but only if he were given complete control. Hindenburg refused.

Papen had no more luck fashioning a majority in the Reichstag than had Brüning. On November 17 he resigned as chancellor but at Hindenburg's request agreed to remain in office until a new government could be formed. Schleicher now wanted the chancellor's job for himself. He had decided that only he was capable of controlling the Nazis, which he proposed to do by dividing the party.

Adolf Hitler was so forceful in his ideas and his opinions that it was rare that anyone dared to oppose or contradict him face-to-face. In *Hitler: A Study in Tyranny*, Allan Bullock quotes two examples of the extent to which the Nazi leader dominated those around him.

Admiral Karl Dönitz, commander of the German navy, confessed,

> I purposely went very seldom to his [Hitler's] headquarters, for I had the feeling that I would thus best preserve my power of initiative, and also because, after several days at headquarters, I always had the feeling that I had to disengage myself from his power of suggestion. I am telling you this because in this connexion I was doubtless more fortunate than his Staff, who were constantly exposed to his power and personality.

Even those closest to Hitler—the most powerful men in the Nazi Party—hesitated to say anything to contradict their führer. Hjalmar Schacht, the minister of economics, recalled,

> On one occasion I managed to persuade [Hermann] Göring to use his influence on Hitler to put on the brake in some economic matter or other only to learn afterward that he had not dared raise the question after all. When I reproached him he replied: "I often make up my mind to say something to him, but then when I come face to face with him my heart sinks into my boots.

Schleicher became chancellor on December 2 and offered the vice-chancellorship to Gregor Strasser, who had remained a Nazi despite his many disagreements with Hitler.

Hitler heard of the offer and called a meeting of party leaders. He berated Strasser for what he termed disloyalty. Two days later, Strasser resigned from the party, and Hitler worried that the more liberal Nazis might follow him. "He [Hitler] is embittered and deeply wounded by [Strasser's] treachery," wrote Goebbels. "Finally he stops and says: If the party once falls to pieces I'll put an end to it all in three minutes with a pistol shot."[50]

Hitler need not have worried. Strasser, deciding he lacked the power to challenge Hitler, withdrew from politics altogether. Schleicher's plan had failed. He had expected at least sixty Nazi Reichstag members to support Strasser. None did. Schleicher now found himself in the same position as Brüning and Papen—unable to form an effective majority and having to resort to presidential decree.

Hitler and Papen

Papen, feeling betrayed by Schleicher, resolved to bring him down and put himself back in power. He still had the ear of Hindenburg, a close friend. He decided to join forces with the Nazis to overthrow Schleicher. On January 4, 1933, Hitler and Papen held the first of several secret meetings at which they agreed to a partnership between the Nazis and the National People's Party. Over the next few weeks Papen had several talks with Hindenburg, gradually convincing the president that Schleicher was losing support. As a result, when Schleicher asked Hindenburg on January 28 to dissolve the Reichstag and call new elections, the president refused. Schleicher resigned, and Hindenburg asked Papen to form a government.

Papen realized that he needed the support of the Nazis and that Hitler would not be satisfied with anything except the chancellorship. Hindenburg was reluctant. Only a week earlier he had told a group of army officers, "Gentlemen, surely you do not think that I would appoint this Austrian corporal Chancellor of Germany."[51] Papen overcame his doubts. Hitler would be chancellor, he told Hindenburg, but Nazis would hold only two other positions in the eleven-member cabinet: Wilhelm Frick as minister of the interior and Göring as interior minister of Prussia. General Werner von Blomberg, who was to be minister of defense, assured Hindenburg that the army would remain loyal. Hindenburg gave in.

At 11 A.M. on January 30, Hitler received a summons to Hindenburg's office. Across the street in the Kaiserhof Hotel, the top Nazis waited. Goebbels wrote in his diary:

What is happening there? We are torn between doubt, hope, joy and despair. We have been deceived too often to be able whole-heartedly to believe in the great miracle. . . . We shall be able to judge by his face if the interview was happy. . . . At last a car draws up in front of the entrance. . . . A few moments later he is with us. He says nothing, and we all remain silent also. His eyes are full of tears. It has come! The Führer is appointed chancellor.[52]

Hitler immediately set about consolidating his power. On February 5, claiming the Nationalists had made impossible demands, he got Hindenburg to dissolve the Reichstag and call new elections for March 5. A week before election day, the Reichstag building burned to the ground. Martin van der Lubbe, a simpleminded Dutch Communist, was found in the ruins and arrested. Although never proven, it seems clear that the Nazis knew of his plan and even had placed storm troopers in the building to make sure the job was done properly.

The End of Liberty

Using the Reichstag fire as evidence, Hitler claimed a Communist uprising was imminent. He persuaded Hindenburg on February 28 to sign a decree that gave the government the power to suspend personal liberties, freedom of the press, and the right to assemble; to search persons and houses without a warrant; and to seize property. Over the next few days, thousands of Communists were arrested and thrown into prison. Rallies of liberal and leftist parties were broken up by club-wielding storm troopers.

Also taking part was Department 1-A of the Interior Ministry, now under Göring's control. Until now a police intelligence-gathering unit, its numbers and its responsibilities were to be vastly enlarged by the Nazis, and it was to acquire a new name—the Geheime Staatspolizei, or secret state police, later shortened to Gestapo. It was a name that would terrorize Europe within a few years.

Despite the Nazis' strong-arm tactics, they won only 44 percent of the vote and were denied a clear majority in the Reichstag. Hitler knew he would have to find another way to establish a dictatorship other than through the polls.

On March 23 the new Reichstag met in the Kroll Opera House, its own chambers in ruins from the fire. Nazi banners hung everywhere. Nazi members were all in uniform. Storm troopers lined the walls of the auditorium. Presented for consideration was the "Law for Removing the Distress of People and Reich," also known as the Enabling Act. In five

The Reichstag, gutted by the fire set by Martin van der Lubbe. Many scholars believe the Nazis encouraged and aided Lubbe in his attempt.

paragraphs, the measure took the entire authority of governing—including budget, legislation, and foreign policy—away from the Reichstag and placed it with the cabinet. All laws were to be written by the chancellor and "might deviate from the constitution."[53] A two-thirds vote was necessary to pass the En-

abling Act, but the Nazis had planned carefully. All the Communist delegates had been arrested, and members of other parties had either been threatened or given empty promises.

When the Enabling Act was passed by a vote of 441 to 84, the Nazis jumped to their feet, stretching out their arms in the party salute. Hitler had been made a virtual dictator. Democracy in Germany was dead. Within a week all state governments were dissolved. On May 2 labor unions were disbanded and collective bargaining was outlawed. On July 14 a new law proclaimed that "The National Socialist German Workers' Party constitutes the only political party in Germany."[54]

Party Troubles

In spite of its triumph, all was not well inside the Nazi Party. Its more liberal wing—mostly followers of the deposed Gregor Strasser—demanded that the party now take control of industry, banking, and the army. Furthermore, Röhm proposed that his SA, now numbering about 2.5 million storm troopers, be placed with the army under the Ministry of Defense, which he would head. This Hitler refused to do. Instead, he met secretly with top military officers aboard the navy cruiser *Deutschland*, promising to keep the army independent in exchange for support in his bid to succeed the ailing Hindenburg as president.

In June 1934 Hitler confronted Röhm. The argument lasted more than five hours, with Hitler accusing Röhm of "preparing a national Bolshevist [Communist] action that could bring nothing but untold misfortune to Germany."[55] Röhm accused Hitler of abandoning the revolution and his old comrades. In a public statement two days later, Röhm said, "The SA is and remains the destiny of Germany."[56]

With the situation threatening to erupt into civil war, Hindenburg told Hitler that if matters were not brought under control, he would declare martial law and hand over power to the army. Hitler knew something must be done. He decided to settle old accounts once and for all.

Early on the morning of June 30, Hitler and Goebbels flew to Munich and were driven by an SS escort to a resort hotel at nearby Bad Wiessee, where Röhm and a few of his top SA lieutenants were vacationing. Hitler personally entered Röhm's room and accused him of treason. He gave his former comrade the options of suicide or summary execution, leaving a pistol in the room. "If I am to be killed," sneered Röhm, "let Adolf Hitler do it himself."[57] Two SS officers then shot him at point-blank range.

Settling Old Accounts

The SA leader was by no means Hitler's only victim in what later became known as the Blood Purge or the Night of the Long Knives. General Schleicher and his wife were gunned down. Gregor Strasser was taken to an underground cell and shot dead. Gustav Ritter von Kahr, whom Hitler still blamed for the failure of the Beer Hall Putsch

After Hitler gained power he proceeded to eliminate his enemies, including Ernst Röhm. On June 30, Hitler had Röhm killed by two SS soldiers.

eleven years earlier, was stabbed to death. Father Bernhard Stempfle, a priest who had helped Hitler write *Mein Kampf* and who presumably knew too many of the führer's personal secrets, was found with three bullets in his heart. In all, about eighty-five people were killed and hundreds more imprisoned. Hitler was now absolute master not only of Germany but also of the Nazi Party.

With the Nazis firmly in power and all other political parties outlawed, it was only natural that the party would grow. Between 1933 and 1935, membership jumped 193 percent to almost 2.5 million.

The character of the party changed, as well. Being a Nazi now was not only "respectable" but conferred advantages. If a person wished to further his career, either in government or private business, Nazi membership was almost a must. Consequently, the newer party members tended to be older and more affluent. More than 30 percent of those who joined from 1933 to 1935 were between forty and sixty years of age. More than one-third were either self-employed or in government service. The number of schoolteachers holding Nazi membership, for instance, rose more than 500 percent.

Two months after the Blood Purge, on August 2, 1934, President Hindenburg died. An hour later, the announcement was made that the offices of chancellor and president would be combined. That same day, all German soldiers were required to take an oath to "render unconditional obedience to Adolf Hitler, the Führer of the German nation and people, Supreme Commander of the Armed Forces."[58] The Nazis had completed their seizure of power. They would next turn their attention to the long-standing objects of their hatred—the Jews.

CHAPTER 5

The Nazis and the Jews

Historian Klaus Fischer calls anti-Semitism "the hate that fueled the Nazi movement."[59] In the years leading to Hitler's seizure of power, Jews had suffered sporadic violence at the hands of storm troopers. After 1933, however, the Nazis were able to turn the full machinery of government against their avowed enemies. As a result, the Jews were slowly stripped of rights and property until all that remained were their lives. The Holocaust would take millions of those, as well.

Immediately after Hitler became chancellor, the SA and SS began a campaign of terror against political opponents, especially Jews, hauling thousands away from their families and penning them in concentration camps. The term *concentration camp* had been coined at the beginning of the twentieth century to describe the facilities used by the British to detain South African civilians during the Boer War. Under the Nazis they came to be known as places of horror and brutality from which few returned alive.

At first the concentration camps were small oper-ations, sometimes located in abandoned army barracks, many scattered around Berlin. Some would be shut down, some consolidated; those that remained would be turned by the SS into enormous centers of human suffering. Their names—Dachau, Bergen-Belsen, Ravensbrück, Buchenwald—would echo throughout Europe. Although thousands died there from beatings, disease, and starvation, their function was not mass murder. The so-called death camps would come later.

Fear, apprehension, and resignation can be seen in the faces of these unfortunate concentration camp inmates as they line up for roll call.

Nazi violence against the Jews was immediately condemned by newspapers and politicians in other countries. Convinced the criticism was an international Jewish plot, Hitler ordered a national boycott of Jewish businesses for April 1, 1933. It was an ill-conceived plan. The Nazis had not realized that non-Jewish businesses—those that supplied Jewish firms with supplies, for instance—would also be affected. Prices tumbled on the Berlin stock exchange. Nevertheless, against the advice of government

A woman reads a sign that urges people to boycott Jewish-owned businesses. The boycott was just one of several measures Hitler took to persecute the Jews.

economists, the boycott was implemented. So few people participated that it was canceled after only a few hours.

Anti-Jewish Laws

The Nazis next struck at the Jews through a series of laws designed to exclude them from many professions. Starting on April 7 and continuing through the rest of 1933, the Nazi-dominated Reichstag passed measures banning Jews from civil service careers, including teaching, and also from the legal profession, dentistry, theater and film, from serving as doctors on government boards, and from the mass media. On September 28 a law was enacted that banned Jews or their spouses from any government employment.

At the same time, the Nazis took the first steps toward achieving what they viewed as racial purity. On July 14 the Entitled Law for the Prevention of Progeny with Hereditary Diseases took effect, authorizing forced sterilization for a wide and fairly vague number of reasons, including alcoholism and "feeblemindedness." More than 400,000 persons—including many Germans along with Jews, Gypsies, and other "undesirables"—underwent the procedure.

German Jews had been fearfully watching the Nazi rise to power. The 1933 laws created a panic. More than thirty-seven thousand Jews fled Germany, more than in any other pre–World War II year except 1939. In 1934 about sixteen thousand returned, disillusioned with their lives as refugees in other countries or encouraged by a lessening of Nazi terror.

Though 1934 was indeed a better year for German Jews, mainly because Hitler was occupied putting the Nazi Party in order,

This Jewish family was part of the mass exodus of Jews from Germany in 1933. Barred from entering Palestine, they wandered for two months until finally being accepted for immigration by Poland.

there were some ominous behind-the-scenes developments. After the Blood Purge, the SS became independent of the SA and Himmler began reporting directly to Hitler. The Gestapo was taken from under Göring and also placed under Himmler. To complete the transformation of Germany into a police state, the *Sicherheitsdienst*, or security service, better known as the SD, was formed. "The SD," Himmler said, "will discover the enemies of the National Socialist concept and it will initiate countermeasures through the official police authorities."[60] Anyone suspected of being anti-Nazi would come under SD surveillance and could be arrested at any time and sent to a concentration camp without trial.

Reinhard Heydrich

Commanding the SD was Reinhard Heydrich, who had served in the German navy but had been court-martialed in 1931. He joined the SS the next year and quickly impressed Himmler, who assigned him a major role in the Blood Purge. It is possible that Heydrich had at least one Jewish ancestor, although he furiously denied it and filed lawsuits against anyone who mentioned it. Perhaps feeling that his blood might be "tainted" led him to become one of the most ruthless of the Nazis in his persecution of the Jews. It would be Heydrich who would later be assigned to carry out major operations of the Holocaust.

In 1934, however, the Holocaust was far in the future. The Nazis had no clear plan of how to solve what they called the "Jewish problem." In 1933, for instance, Hans Frank, the Nazis' chief lawyer, could say with sincerity, "In this struggle against the Jews, a certain arrangement has been reached . . . and the life and security of the Jews in Germany will not be endangered."[61] The arrangement the Nazis had in mind was that Jews would be strictly segregated from Germans socially, in the workplace, and in legal status. This was expressed in 1935 in the so-called "Nuremberg Laws," presented on September 15 at the annual Nazi rally.

The Nuremberg Laws fixed into law the inferior status of the Jews and attempted to prevent them from "polluting" German blood. The first law, the Law for the Protection of German Blood and German Honor, forbade either marriage or sexual relations between Jews and Germans and banned the employment in Jewish homes of any German female under forty-five years of age. The second law, the Reich Citizenship Law, denied German citizenship to Jews and gave them instead the status of "subjects."

Known as the hangman for his role in the Blood Purge, Reinhard Heydrich would later head the plan to solve the "Jewish problem."

The "Jewish Problem"

No hard evidence exists to support the claims of some scholars that the Nazis intended from the first to exterminate the Jews of Europe. Instead, Nazi policy toward the Jews went through several stages. At first, laws were passed stripping the Jews of their civil rights and confiscating their property with the idea that they could continue to live in Germany, but be separated from normal society.

Later, it was thought that the best solution to what the Nazis called the "Jewish problem" would be to force all Jews to leave the country. Only later was the possibility of extermination discussed. One of the first mentions of such a measure was in this passage from an SS journal. It is quoted in Yehuda Bauer's *A History of the Holocaust*.

We shall bring the Jewish problem to its complete solution, because it is essential, because we will no longer listen to the outcry in the world, and because actually there is no longer any force in the world that can prevent us from doing so. The plan is clear: total removal, total separation. What does this mean? This means not only the removal of the Jews from the economy of the German people, which they damage by their murderous attacks and their incitement to war and to murder. It means much more than that! No German should be asked to live under the same roof with Jews, who are a race marked as murderers and criminals, and who are the mortal enemies of the German people. Therefore, we must expel the Jews from our houses and our living areas and house them in separate blocks or streets, where they will live among themselves with as little contact with Germans as possible. They should be marked by a special outward mark, and they should be forbidden to own houses or land, or be partners in any such ownership in Germany. . . . But let nobody imagine that we can view such a development [Jews' remaining in Germany] with equanimity [peace of mind]. The German people have no wish to suffer in their midst hundreds of thousands of criminals, who not only maintain themselves by their crime but will also want to take revenge. . . . We would be faced with the hard necessity of exterminating the Jewish underworld in the way we generally exterminate crime in our well-ordered state: with fire and sword. The result would be the actual and final end of Jewry in Germany, its complete destruction.

The Nuremberg Laws did not specify, however, who was legally a Jew. This was decided in a November decree that proclaimed anyone descended from three or more Jewish grandparents to be a "full Jew." Persons were also full Jews if they had two Jewish grandparents and either practiced the Jewish religion, were married to a Jew, or were children born after September 15, 1935, to one Jewish parent and one German parent. Other part-German, part-Jews were designated as *mischlinge*, or half-breeds. While *mischlinge* were denied full rights of citizenship, they were at least later able to escape extermination.

Jewish Reaction

Jewish reaction to the Nuremberg Laws was mixed. Some concluded there was no longer any future for Jews in Germany: Emigration jumped from twenty-one thousand in 1935 to twenty-five thousand in 1936. Others

---

The Resolve of the Jews

As the strength of the Nazis in Germany was growing, most of the country's Jews never thought that the party's anti-Semitic views would have a lasting effect. They thought that clearer heads would prevail and that the Nazi movement would either fail altogether, be absorbed in a consolidation of parties, or mature in its outlook. The actions of the Nazis after 1933, however, woke the Jews to their danger and forced them to take a stand for their religion. The following quotations are from Yehuda Bauer's *A History of the Holocaust*.

Robert Wetsch, a leader of the German Zionists, an organization that advocated the Jews' return to a homeland in Palestine, wrote:

> The first of April, 1933, [the date of a boycott of Jewish businesses] will remain an important date in the history of German Jewry—indeed, in the history of the entire Jewish people. . . . Today the Jews cannot speak except as Jews. Anything else is utterly senseless. . . . Gone is the fatal misapprehension of many Jews that Jewish interests can be pressed under some cover. . . . April 1, 1933, can become the day of Jewish awakening and Jewish rebirth. If the Jews will it. If the Jews are mature and

have greatness in them. . . . A powerful symbol is to be found in the fact that the boycott leadership gave orders that a sign "with a yellow badge on a black background" was to be pasted on the boycotted shops. This regulation is intended as a brand, a sign of contempt. We will take it up and make of it a badge of honor.

An anti-Zionist Jewish newspaper echoed the same sentiment:

> The purpose of a community reveals itself in times of trouble. When the individual can no longer see any sense in his existence, when he is alone, the community can direct him to a purpose and an aim; when he alone can no longer do anything, then the community must show its strength. In times of distress the community must grow anew, gain life and existence. . . . Let nobody fail in his duty in this hour of trial! Let everybody contribute according to his ability, and in his own place, to the task of helping others! The hour of German Jewry has arrived, the hour of responsibility, the hour of trial. Let German Jewry prove itself capable of facing this hour.

almost welcomed the laws because at least they seemed to resolve the status of the Jews and allowed them to remain in Germany, though as noncitizens. A group that spoke for most German Jews published this rationalization:

> The laws passed in the Reichstag at Nuremberg hit the Jews of Germany very hard, but they are designed to create a basis that will enable tolerable relations to develop between the German nation and the Jewish nation. . . . A precondition for "tolerable relations" is the hope that the cessation of destruction and boycott may make moral and economic existence possible for Jews and their communities in Germany.[62]

The Nazis were divided on how to deal with the Jews. The more radical Nazis, such as Streicher and Goebbels, wanted to continue a program of physical terror. The conservatives were afraid of the effect such tactics might have on both foreign relations and the economy. Hitler, for the time being, sided with the latter view and insisted that repression of the Jews occur through "legal" means.

Meanwhile, the Jews were suffering persecution other than that sanctioned by law. The German public, under a steady barrage of anti-Semitic propaganda from the Nazis, began to practice unofficial forms of discrimination. Jews were harassed when they tried to enter restaurants and other public places. Shops posted signs in their windows saying Jewish customers were not welcome. On a road outside one village a sign read, "Drive Carefully! Sharp Curve! Jews 75 Miles an Hour!"[63]

The Jews received some relief in 1936 when the summer Olympic Games were staged in Berlin. Hitler wanted the world, including the news media, to see Nazi Germany as a place of law, order, peace. Accordingly, anti-Semitic slogans were taken down or painted over, police were under strict orders not to harass Jews in the streets or to allow others to do so, and the SA and SS kept a low profile. As a result, many visitors left Germany favorably impressed with the Third Reich and believing that the stories they had heard had been, as the Nazis claimed, Jewish lies.

The last Olympic runner sprints to light the Olympic flame in Berlin. The Olympics brought a brief respite for Jews; the Nazis had to conceal their institutionalized anti-Semitism from international visitors.

The Four-Year Plan

The respite brought about by the Olympic Games was brief. On September 9, 1936, Hitler proclaimed a Four-Year Plan to reform the German economy. In announcing that "Germany must be wholly independent of foreign areas in those materials which can be produced in any way through German ability," Hitler was already looking forward to a war through which Germany would seize its "living space." [64]

One part of the Four-Year Plan, although not publicly announced, was the systematic takeover of Jewish businesses and property. This policy served two purposes: to enrich the top Nazis and their friends and to prevent Jews from taking wealth out of the country. The usual method of taking over a business was to make it nearly impossible to do business through discriminatory laws, thereby forcing the owner to sell at a low price. The process was known as Aryanization, and while it was supposed to redistribute Jewish assets evenly throughout Germany, the only ones to benefit were the Nazis. Göring, who was in charge of the Four-Year Plan, grew fabulously wealthy as a result.

In addition, Jews who wanted to leave Germany had to pay a "flight tax," normally one-fourth of all their assets. Such extortion was a big moneymaker for the Nazis, bringing in the equivalent of $132 million in 1938–1939. Moreover, those who left had to exchange their Reichmarks for the currencies of the countries to which they were going, always at vastly inflated rates of exchange. These regulations had the effect of discouraging the wealthier Jews from emigrating.

Economic considerations aside, the German Jews had strong personal ties to their country. They considered themselves good, loyal Germans. In 1933 a group of Jewish leaders wrote to Hitler:

We have learned to love the German soil. It contains the graves of our ancestors. . . . Our link with this soil goes back through history for 2,000 years. . . . And we have learned to love the German people. At times it hurt us, particularly in the Middle Ages. But we were also present at its rise. We feel closely linked to its culture. It has become a part of our intellectual being and has given us German Jews a stamp [character] of our own. [65]

Many Jews reasoned that they could ride out the storm. It might be bad for a few years, they thought, but the Nazis could not last forever. Almost no one could foresee that persecution would evolve into genocide.

Kristallnacht

Still, most Jews thought they were safe. They were made to think otherwise on the night of November 9, 1938. Three days earlier, a German diplomat in Paris had been assassinated by a young Polish Jew whose parents had been put in a concentration camp. The Nazis used the incident to unleash an unprecedented night of terror against Jews throughout Germany. The plan was suggested by Goebbels and approved by Hitler, who said, "The SA should be allowed to have a fling." [66]

The riots, supposedly spontaneous, had actually been carefully organized by Heydrich. Instructions specified that "As many Jews, especially rich ones, are to be arrested as can be accommodated in the existing prisons." [67] The Nazi storm troopers went on a rampage, burning and looting thousands of Jewish shops and burning most synagogues to the ground. Hundreds of Jews were beaten, and at least thirty-six were killed. More than twenty thousand were hauled off to concentration camps. So

Some of the devastation wreaked upon the Jews in the aftermath of Kristallnacht.

much broken glass littered the streets of German cities that the night was known as *Kristallnacht*, or Night of Broken Glass. The final insult came when the Nazis blamed the Jews for all the damage. All insurance mon-

ey due to them was confiscated. In addition, they were fined a billion marks "for their abominable crimes."[68]

Of the estimated 522,000 Jews in Germany in 1933, about 130,000 had fled by the

Kristallnacht

On the night of November 9, 1938, members of the Nazi SA and SS unleashed a rampage of terror against the Jews of Germany. Synagogues were burned, shops smashed, and innocent people beaten and killed.

The riots, supposedly spontaneous outbreaks, were actually carefully planned by Joseph Goebbels with Hitler's approval. This account of what came to be known as *Kristallnacht*, the Night of Broken Glass, was published on November 10, 1938, in the *New York Times*. It was reprinted in the *Record*, a publication of the Anti-Defamation League of B'nai B'rith, a worldwide Jewish organization, in 1978.

BERLIN, Nov. 10—A wave of destruction, looting and incendiarism unparalleled in Germany since the Thirty Years War and in Europe generally since the Bolshevist revolution, swept over Great Germany today as National Socialist cohorts [groups] took vengeance on Jewish shops, offices and synagogues for the murder by a young Polish Jew of Ernst von Rath, third secretary of the German Embassy in Paris.

Beginning systematically in the early morning hours in almost every town and city in the country, the wrecking, looting and burning continued all day. Huge but mostly silent crowds looked on and the police confined themselves to regulating traffic and making wholesale arrests of Jews "for their own protection."

All day the main shopping districts as well as the side streets of Berlin and innumerable other places resounded to the shattering of shop windows falling to the pavement, the dull thuds of furniture and fittings being pounded to pieces and the clamor of fire brigades rushing to burning shops and synagogues. Although shop fires were quickly extinguished, synagogue fires were merely kept from spreading to adjoining buildings.

. . . Generally the crowds were silent and the majority seemed gravely disturbed by the proceedings. Only members of the wrecking squads shouted occasionally, "Perish Jewry!" and "Kill the Jews!" and in one case a person in the crowd shouted, "Why not hang the owner in the window?"

end of 1937. *Kristallnacht* woke most of the remainder from their dream of coexistence with the Nazis. In 1938–1939, about 100,000 Jews left Germany and another 116,000 emigrated from Austria, which had been annexed by Germany in March 1938. This suited the Nazis perfectly. In fact, they had begun a program of forced emigration in an effort to rid the Third Reich of all its Jews.

Adolf Eichmann

In charge of the program was a thirty-three-year-old SS officer named Adolf Eichmann. Eichmann had grown up in Linz, Austria, the same village where Hitler had spent his youth. He was a shy and lonely boy, and nicknamed "the little Jew" by playmates because of his dark complexion. Later, in Vienna, he began attending Nazi meetings and joined the party in 1933. After moving to Germany, he joined Heydrich's SD and became its expert as the head of the notorious Section IV-B-4, the office of "Jewish Affairs." In 1942 Eichmann would be responsible for rounding up Jews from throughout Nazi-occupied Europe and shipping them to the death camps.

The problem with the forced emigration of German and Austrian Jews was that few countries were willing to accept them in large numbers. Some feared that a sudden wave of immigrants would compete with native citizens for jobs. Others closed their doors simply because of anti-Semitism. In July 1938 representatives of twenty-nine countries met at Evian, France, at a conference called by American president Franklin Roosevelt. Most came prepared to say, not what they could do for the Jews, but what they would not do. The United States refused to discuss its immigration limits. The British refused to discuss Palestine, which it had controlled since World War I.

From 1933 to 1936, the British government had supported the Zionists, members of a movement committed to bringing large numbers of Jews to Palestine to form a Jewish homeland. The number of immigrants was limited to what the British thought the economy of Palestine could support, but even so, about 171,000 Jews were admitted during these years.

In 1936, however, Arab leaders, alarmed by the influx of Jews, pressured the British government into withdrawing its support of the Zionist movement. As a result, a total of only about 25,000 Jews were legally admitted to Palestine in 1937 and 1938. The Zionists turned to smuggling Jews to Palestine, but the numbers were far smaller.

When World War II broke out in 1939, forced emigration of Jews from Germany was no longer an option for the Nazis. In 1940 the Germans proposed a plan by which all Jews would be moved to the island of Madagascar off the east coast of Africa. The "Madagascar Plan" was never implemented for two reasons. First, there was no practical way to ship millions of people, especially in wartime. Second, the Nazi-occupied countries of eastern Europe, in which the Germans sought their *lebensraum*, held far more Jews than Madagascar could accommodate.

German and Czechoslovakian Jews arrive in France after fleeing Germany. German Jews had a difficult time immigrating because other nations refused to accept them.

The Final Solution

The Nazi policy against the Jews had progressed from legal repression to seizure of property to forced emigration. The next phase would be to force the Jews of Germany, Austria, and the conquered portions of eastern Europe and the Soviet Union into concentration camps or pack them into ghettos, special sections of a city where huge numbers of people were forced to live, usually in squalid conditions. When that was accomplished, the stage would be set for the *endlösung*—the "final solution" of the "Jewish problem." Hitler had left no doubt what that would be. In February 1939 he said in a speech:

During the time of my struggle for power it was in the first instance only the Jewish race that received my prophecies with laughter when I said that I would one day take over the leadership of the State . . . and that I would then among other things settle the Jewish problem. Their laughter was uproarious, but I think that for some time now they have been laughing on the other side of their face. Today I will once more be a prophet: if they [Jews] succeed in plunging the nations once more into a world war, then the result [will be] the annihilation of the Jewish race in Europe.[69]

CHAPTER 6

War and Destruction

In *Mein Kampf*, Adolf Hitler set forth his goals with unmistakable clarity: to unite the German *Völk* into a single nation and to secure *lebensraum* in the lands to the east. It should have come as no surprise to the rest of the world when the Nazi leader, step by step, moved in exactly that direction. When other nations finally tried to stop him, the result was World War II and the Holocaust.

Hitler boasted that his empire would last a thousand years. It would in fact last only sixty-eight months, but in that brief time 55 million people would be killed in battle, by bombing, and in the death camps created by the Nazis to carry out their doctrine of racial purity. Germany would be pulled into a war it could not win and one that would eventually result in the Nazis' annihilation.

When Hitler took power in 1933, Germany was militarily weak. Her army had been limited to 100,000 soldiers by the Versailles treaty and her munitions had been surrendered. She was limited to thirty-six ships in her navy and her air force had been abolished altogether. It was no wonder, then, that Hitler tried to convey the impression that all he and Germany wanted was peace and security, not war. Nevertheless, on October 14 he announced that Germany would withdraw from the disarmament conference being conducted in Geneva, Switzer-

land, and would withdraw from the League of Nations, as well.

In 1934 Hitler attempted to foster a good relationship with Italian dictator Benito Mussolini, but Mussolini distrusted the Nazi leader. He knew Hitler wanted eventually to unite all people of German origin into a single nation and was afraid this would include the South Tyrol, an area of Austria that had been given to Italy after World War I.

The Nazis' fortunes took a turn for the better early in 1935 when the citizens of the Saar region on Germany's southwestern border with France voted overwhelmingly to be reunited with Germany. Hitler followed by announcing the formation of the Luftwaffe—the German air force—the resumption of a military draft, and an increase in the army's strength to 550,000 men. Although these actions were direct violations of the Versailles treaty, the other nations of Europe did nothing.

Later in the year, relations improved between Germany and Italy. In October, Mussolini, having told the Italian people he would fashion a new Roman empire, invaded Ethiopia in northern Africa. Britain and France demanded that the League of Nations impose sanctions on Italy. Meanwhile, Hitler voiced support of the Italian invasion, thereby earning Mussolini's gratitude at the same

Hitler and Mussolini pose on a balcony in Venice in 1934. Originally suspicious of Hitler, Mussolini joined forces with him after Hitler did not protest Mussolini's invasion of Ethiopia.

time Britain and France were making him an enemy.

March into the Rhineland

Hitler now made his boldest move yet. He decided to test the great powers of Europe by sending German troops into the Rhineland, the part of Germany on its western border with France that the Versailles treaty had specifically stated was to be free of armed forces. Hitler's generals knew that if the far stronger French army marched against them, they would be forced to make a humiliating retreat. Hitler held firm.

On March 7, 1936, twenty-two thousand German troops marched into the Rhineland and occupied key positions near the French border. The French and British did nothing. Even Hitler had known the extent of the gamble he was taking. Later, he said, "The forty-eight hours after the march into the Rhineland were the most nerve-racking in my life. If the French had then marched into the Rhineland we would have had to withdraw with our tails between our legs, for the military resources at our disposal would have been wholly inadequate."[70]

Once more the other European powers had stood by as Hitler violated the Versailles treaty. One English diplomat, Lord Lothian, even said, "The Germans, after all, are only going into their own back yard."[71]

The March into the Rhineland

The boldest move in Hitler's career and the one that showed him that the western European powers—France and Great Britain—lacked the will to oppose him came in 1936 when German troops marched into the Rhineland. Under the provisions of the Treaty of Versailles, this area in western Germany was to remain free of troops and to act as a buffer zone between Germany and France.

On March 7, 1936, Hitler announced the rearmament of the Rhineland to the Reichstag. William Shirer witnessed the speech and quoted his own journal account in *The Rise and Fall of the Third Reich*.

"In the interest [Hitler said] of the primitive rights of its people to the security of their frontier and the safeguarding of their defense, the German government has re-established, as from today, the absolute and unrestricted sovereignty of the Reich in the demilitarized zone." Now the six hundred deputies, personal appointees all of Hitler, little men with big bodies and bulging necks and cropped hair and pouched bellies and brown uniforms and heavy boots . . . leap to their feet like automatons, their right arms upstretched in the Nazi salute, and scream, "Heils" . . . Hitler raises his hand for silence. . . . He says in a deep, resonant voice, "Men of the Reichstag!" The silence is utter. "In this historic hour, when, in the Reich's western provinces, German troops are at this minute marching into their future peacetime garrisons, we shall all unite in two sacred vows." He can go no further. . . . All the militarism in [the deputies'] German blood surges to their heads. They spring, yelling and crying, to their feet. . . . Their hands are raised in slavish salute, their faces now contorted with hysteria, their mouths wide open, shouting, shouting, their eyes, burning with fanaticism, glued on the new god, the Messiah.

Children in Cologne, Germany, enthusiastically greet German soldiers during the reoccupation of the Rhineland.

Hitler had learned just how much Britain and France would yield to avoid war. Furthermore, the nations to the east of Germany—Poland and Czechoslovakia—were suddenly afraid that their treaties with France might not mean much if Hitler turned against them.

On October 21 Germany and Italy signed a secret agreement outlining cooperation in foreign affairs. Three days later, Hitler told Mussolini's son-in-law that Germany and Italy together could conquer Europe. "In three years," he said, "Germany will be ready."[72] In December, Göring told a group of high officials, "We are already on the threshold of mobilization and we are already at war. All that is lacking is the actual shooting."[73]

Throughout 1937 Hitler hammered away at his goal of uniting all Germanic people in a single nation. In a meeting with British diplomat Lord Halifax he made it clear that he was seeking to unite Germany and Austria. Furthermore, he protested what he called the brutal treatment of the large German population in the Sudetenland, an area of northwestern Czechoslovakia, and mentioned the possibility of having to intervene there. Halifax replied that Britain was willing to explore any solution that did not involve military force.

The Seizure of Austria

In 1938, having already extracted Mussolini's promise that he would not interfere, Hitler was convinced that he was free to act against Austria. A strong Nazi-backed opposition party there advocated annexation by Germany. In February the chancel-

When Austrian chancellor Kurt von Schuschnigg opposed Hitler's takeover of his country, the führer responded by taking the country by force.

lor of Austria, Kurt von Schuschnigg, feeling increasingly abandoned by his allies, met with Hitler in Germany. He was presented a draft of an agreement lifting a ban on the Nazi Party and giving Nazis key positions in the Austrian cabinet. When Schuschnigg tried to negotiate, Hitler said the terms were final and that the German army would march into Austria if Schuschnigg did not sign immediately. Demoralized, Schuschnigg agreed to sign.

After he returned to Austria, Schuschnigg decided on one last attempt to keep his country independent of Germany. On March 9 he announced that there would be a national election on March 13 in which Austrians would be asked whether or not they wanted to remain free. Hitler was furious. He could not run the risk of a public vote against annexation and was determined to prevent the election from taking place.

On March 12 German tanks rolled across the border with Hitler in personal command. He paused in his boyhood home of Linz to make a speech, saying, "If Providence once called me forth from this town to be the leader of the Reich, it must in so doing have charged me with a mission, and that mission could only be to restore my dear homeland to the German Reich."[74] Two days later, as flower-waving crowds lined streets hung with Nazi banners, Hitler rode in triumph through Vienna, where he had once lived as a vagrant.

The first Austrians to suffer under their new masters were the Jews. Anti-Semitism had been even stronger in Austria than in Germany because of its larger Jewish popula-

tion. Within days of the Nazi takeover, thousands of Jews were arrested. Some were forced to clean the streets on their hands and knees while storm troopers stood guard and Viennese jeered. Others were forced to clean the latrines of the SA and SS. Eichmann's emigration office did a brisk business as the Jews who had enough money hastened to buy their way out of the country.

Czechoslovakia, now almost surrounded on three sides by Germany, was Hitler's next target. Throughout the summer of 1938 the Nazis kept up a torrent of propaganda claiming the Sudeten Germans were receiving outrageous treatment at the hands of the

Jews are forced to clean the streets of Vienna in 1938. Hitler and his SS imposed this sort of humiliation on Jews after taking over the countries in which they lived.

Czechs. The crisis built until it seemed war was inevitable. At last Hitler delivered an ultimatum, saying if the Sudetenland were not returned to Germany by October 1, his army would invade.

The Munich Conference

British prime minister Neville Chamberlain, determined to prevent war, flew to Germany on September 15 to confer with Hitler. Hitler would not budge from his demands. Mussolini, afraid of being dragged into a general war for which his country was not prepared, appealed to Hitler to reconsider. Reluctantly, Hitler agreed that the Czechoslovakian question would be settled at a conference on September 29 at Munich.

The proposal presented by Britain and France at the conference was essentially the same set of demands Hitler had presented Chamberlain in September. The only changes were that a few areas of the Sudetenland were not to be occupied until later than previously demanded and that an international commission was to decide where the borders would be drawn. Two Czech representatives waiting in another room protested these terms. "If you do not accept," they were told, "you will have to settle your affairs with the Germans absolutely alone." [75]

The next day, Chamberlain presented Hitler with a short statement saying that the Munich agreement symbolized Germany's and Britain's promise never to go to war with one another. Hitler read it quickly and signed it. On his return to England, Chamberlain waved the statement to a cheering crowd, later declaring, "I believe it is peace in our time." [76]

Hitler lost no time in ignoring the Munich agreement. The "international commission" was dominated by Germany and drew the new borders exactly as Hitler wanted. The Nazi leader then pressured two large Czechoslovakian minorities, the Slovaks and the Ruthenians, into demanding their own independent countries that would be controlled by Germany. When the president of Czechoslovakia appealed to Hitler, he was told that if he did not surrender his country to Germany, it would be invaded. The president gave in, and a document was signed.

The surrender of Czechoslovakia finally woke the British and French to the danger of their situation. They had deceived themselves into thinking that Hitler wanted only to unite people of German origin. By swallowing Czechoslovakia, he had demonstrated his real intention—to dominate all of Europe.

The next target of the Nazis was Poland. The Treaty of Versailles had split East Prussia from the rest of Germany. In between was the Polish Corridor, a slender strip of land running north from Poland to the Baltic Sea port of Danzig. Once the Czechoslovakian question was settled, German foreign minister Joachim von Ribbentrop presented Polish foreign minister Jozef Beck with a demand that Danzig be returned and a highway be built to link it with Germany.

Britain Supports Poland

Beck turned down the Nazis' demands and received support from Britain when Chamberlain, finally recognizing the German threat, announced on March 31, 1939, that Britain would unconditionally support Poland if it were attacked. Hitler went into a rage, shouting, "I'll cook them [the British] a stew they'll choke on." [77] On April 3, he sent directives to his top generals instructing them to prepare for an invasion of Poland to take place on September 1.

The German army rolls into Prague in March 1939. The Nazi takeover of Czechoslovakia was made possible by the reluctance of Great Britain and France to risk the war with Germany.

Before launching such an attack, however, Hitler had to make sure that if he did invade Poland he would not be fighting Britain, France, and the Soviet Union at the same time. Hitler had been the sworn enemy of Communist Russia for decades. Negotiating with Joseph Stalin, dictator of the Soviet Union, violated everything he had preached, but Hitler knew Stalin did not want to be pulled into a war on the side of Britain and France, whom he regarded with distrust and suspicion. After months of delicate negotiations, on August 23, Stalin signed a nonaggression treaty effective for ten years.

The way was now open for Hitler to invade Poland. On the night of August 31, SS men in Polish uniforms seized a radio station at Gleiwitz on the German side of the border. After broadcasting some anti-German slogans and firing a few shots, they withdrew, leaving behind them the corpses of some concentration camp prisoners dressed in Polish uniforms. Using this charade as an excuse, Germany invaded Poland the next day. Two days later, Britain and France declared war on Germany, beginning World War II. A month later, Hitler signed an order permitting doctors to give lethal injections for the "destruction of unproductive lives."[78] The Holocaust had begun.

On the morning of September 1, 1939, Germany unleashed a new kind of warfare—

blitzkrieg, or lightning war. Within two weeks, Poland had disappeared. Germany grabbed the western half, and the Soviet Union, under the secret terms of the nonaggression pact with Hitler, took the eastern half.

Britain and France were stunned by the fate of Poland. Instead of invading Germany from the west, they did nothing. The French sat behind the Maginot Line, the supposedly impregnable string of forts on their eastern border. The eight months in

Hitler smiles as his troops march into Poland. Hitler's first conquests were met with little opposition.

"What Now?"

There was little doubt that Adolf Hitler wanted war, expected war, and, in fact, would settle for nothing less. From 1936, when Nazi troops marched into the demilitarized Rhineland, to 1938, when Hitler took over Czechoslovakia, he had practically dared Great Britain and France to declare war on Germany.

Nevertheless, when Great Britain stood by its guarantees to Poland and declared war on Germany on September 3, 1939, it seemed to come as a shock to the Nazi leader. Perhaps he thought that the British would back down, as they had done so many times before. Perhaps the finality of what he had led Germany into disturbed him, if only momentarily.

Paul Schmidt, who acted as interpreter between Hitler and the British ambassador, Sir Neville Henderson, remembered taking Hitler an ultimatum from the British government warning that if the attack on Poland were not stopped by 11 A.M. that day (September 3), Britain and Germany would be at war. Schmidt's account is quoted in Allan Bullock's *Hitler: A Study in Tyranny*.

Hitler was sitting at his desk and [Foreign Minister Joachim] Ribbentrop stood by the window. Both looked up expectantly as I came in. I stopped at some distance from Hitler's desk, and then slowly translated the British Government's ultimatum. When I finished, there was complete silence. Hitler sat immobile, gazing before him. He was not at a loss, as was afterwards stated, nor did he rage as others allege. He sat completely silent and unmoving. After an interval, which seemed like an age, he turned to Ribbentrop, who had remained standing by the window. "What now?" asked Hitler with a savage look, as though implying that his Foreign Minister had misled him about England's probable reaction.

Shortly afterward, Hermann Göring said, "If we lose this war, then God help us."

---

which no fighting took place was known in Germany as the *sitzkrieg*—"sitting war."

Attack in the West

At last, on May 10, 1940, Hitler felt strong enough to attack. Instead of trying to pierce the Maginot Line, the Germans simply went around it, smashing through Belgium, the Netherlands, and Luxembourg without bothering to declare war. France lasted only three weeks longer than had Poland. On June 21 Hitler humiliated the French by forcing them to sign a surrender near the town of Compiègne in the same railroad car in which the Germans had signed the armistice ending World War I. William Shirer, an American journalist who witnessed the scene, reported that the strutting Hitler "throws his whole body into harmony with his mood. He swiftly snaps his hands on his hips, arches his shoulders, plants his feet wide apart. It is a magnificent gesture of defiance."[79]

The conquest of France was the zenith of
[Hitle]r's career and the peak of popularity for
[the N]azis among the German people. The
[Germ]ans had not greeted the outbreak of war
[in 19]39 with great enthusiasm. With the fall
[of Fra]nce, however, Germany was gripped by
pride and patriotism. The quick victories and
the steady stream of Nazi propaganda had
made Hitler a virtual god in the eyes of the
people, who flocked to his every public
appearance, screaming "Heil, Hitler" and
extending their arms in the Nazi salute.

Hitler poses in front of the Eiffel Tower after the fall of France. France surrendered after only six weeks of fighting.

The Technological Dictatorship

Hitler's success in building the Nazi Party into an all-powerful organ that would control every aspect of life in Germany was based on two mechanisms: propaganda and terrorism. Both made use of the mass media to an extent never before seen.

Albert Speer, Nazi minister of armaments, said during his war crimes trial that Hitler's was the first dictatorship to use technology to the fullest. His speech is quoted in Allan Bullock's *Hitler: A Study in Tyranny.*

Hitler's dictatorship differed in one fundamental point from all its predecessors in history. His was the first dictatorship in the present period of modern technical development, a dictatorship which made complete use of all technical means for the domination of its own country. Through technical devices like the radio and the loud speaker, eighty million people were deprived of independent thought. It was thereby possible to subject them to the will of one man. . . . Earlier dictators needed highly qualified assistants, even at the lowest level, men who could think and act independently. The totalitarian system in the period of modern technical development can dispense with them; the means of communication alone make it possible to mechanize the lower leadership. As a result of this there arises the new type of the uncritical recipient of orders. . . . Another result was the far-reaching supervision of the citizens of the State and the maintenance of a high degree of secrecy for criminal acts. The nightmare of many a man that one day nations could be dominated by technical means was all but realized in Hitler's totalitarian system.

The only real opposition to Hitler and the Nazis came from the top ranks of the military. The generals had never gotten used to the idea of taking orders from a former corporal. They were also convinced that a prolonged war would be the ruin of Germany. As early as 1938 groups of conspirators plotted Hitler's overthrow. Every time something happened at the last minute to stop them—they lost their nerve, a stroke of luck saved Hitler, or a great Nazi victory made a successful revolt impossible.

With the fall of France, Great Britain stood alone. Hitler knew that a successful invasion would require German superiority in the air over the English Channel. On August 13, 1940, Göring's Luftwaffe began bombing British airfields, initiating what came to be known as the Battle of Britain.

Britain's Royal Air Force, although much smaller than the Luftwaffe, had two advantages: the skill, bravery, and devotion of its pilots and the use of radar, which the Germans had not yet perfected. The RAF was able to maintain its superiority over the Channel. At last, in November, winter weather made an invasion almost impossible and the invasion was canceled.

London spectators watch the sky as British antiaircraft guns take aim at incoming Luftwaffe bombers. With the help of radar and the determination of the pilots of Britain's Royal Air Force, Germany was never able to achieve air superiority over the skies of England.

The Invasion of Russia

Hitler had never deviated from his vision that Germany's destiny lay in eastward expansion. From the moment the invasion of Great Britain was canceled, men and matériel were shifted in great secrecy from France to the eastern border for an invasion of the Soviet Union. Although Stalin did not trust the Nazis, it nevertheless came as a shock when, on June 22, 1941, 3 million men, 4,000 tanks,

7,000 pieces of artillery, and 3,000 airplanes were launched against his country.

Meanwhile, another invasion had taken place. Special divisions known as *Einsatzgruppen*, or action groups, followed the advancing German troops. Their task was not to fight the Soviet army, but to capture and murder as many Soviet officials, Jews, and Gypsies as possible. In town after town the same scene was repeated. The *Einsatzgruppen* rounded up the Jews and all who they thought might resist, marched them to a remote location, forced them to dig huge pits, then lined them up and mowed them down with machine guns. At Babi Yar, on the outskirts of Kiev, at least 50,000 Ukranians, more than 33,000 of whom were Jews, were murdered on a single September day. By the end of 1941 an estimated 700,000 Jews had been killed.

The mass killings in Russia represented a new kind of warfare—racial war in which genocide instead of military success was the objective. Three months earlier, Hitler had told his top generals what was expected of them and warned the army not to interfere with the SS. He had written:

> This struggle is one of ideologies and racial difference and will have to be conducted with unprecedented, merciless and unrelenting harshness. All officers will have to rid themselves of obsolete ideologies. I know that the necessity for such means of waging war is beyond the comprehension of you generals, but I . . . insist absolutely that my orders be executed without contradiction.[80]

Hitler was never able to engender within the top ranks of the military his passionate hatred of the Jews. The generals showed no great enthusiasm for slaughtering those declared by the führer to be enemies of the *Völk*. The bulk of the mass murders thus were carried out by SS units, although these units contained numerous non-SS personnel from every walk of life who seemed both willing and eager to carry out the Final Solution.

Military Opposition

While the top military leaders, in general, opposed the mass murders, it was not out of any love for the Jews. On the contrary, anti-Semitism was high among the officers. As the Holocaust began and some army units were used against the Jews, the generals worried about the effect on their men's morale, not about the fate of the victims. Later, when the death camps were in operation, the generals'

When Hitler launched Operation Barbarossa, the invasion of the Soviet Union, Stalin was taken by surprise and was forced into a war of attrition.

Stalingrad lies in ruins as a result of German bombs. Hitler's decision to attack the Soviet Union would lead to his defeat.

concern was the number of trains being used to ship Jews to their death rather than carry soldiers to the front.

On December 7, 1941, Japan launched a surprise attack against the U.S. Navy base at Pearl Harbor, Hawaii. Germany was an ally of Japan, formalized in a treaty signed the year before. On December 11, Hitler declared war on the United States.

Hitler's two fateful decisions in 1941—the invasion of the Soviet Union and the declaration of war on the United States—

virtually ensured that Germany would lose World War II. Any chance of an eventual Nazi victory depended on quick conquests, such as those over Poland and France. After 1941 Germany was involved in a long, drawn-out struggle for which it lacked both the manpower and the natural resources.

The year 1942 was a bitter one, both for the Nazis and for the Jews. On January 20 a conference in the Berlin suburb of Wannsee presided over by Heydrich decided that the "final solution" would be the slaughter of every Jew in Europe. Mass executions by poison gas had already been tested in the Polish concentration camp of Auschwitz. The gassings in Auschwitz began full-scale on June 23, and on October 4 orders went out that all Jews in concentration camps were to be sent there.

On the battlefield, meanwhile, the Germans suffered a series of setbacks. Defeats by the British at El Alamein in northern Africa and by the Soviets at Stalingrad marked the beginning of the end. The Germans fared no better in 1943. They were steadily pushed back by the Soviets and completely driven out of North Africa.

Defeat took its toll on Hitler. He developed a facial twitch, and his left arm and leg would occasionally tremble uncontrollably. He made almost no public appearances and gave very few radio speeches. In the face of increasing evidence, he refused to believe

U.S. battleships Oklahoma *and* Maryland *are capsized after the Japanese attack on Pearl Harbor. The attack brought the United States into the war and virtually sealed the doom of Hitler's Third Reich.*

American soldiers happily display a captured Nazi banner in France in 1944. By the time the Allies liberated France, Hitler's dreams of winning the war were lost.

that Germany was losing the war. He refused to visit cities that had been bombed. He would not read gloomy reports from the front. He would fly into a rage, shouting and foaming at the mouth, if anyone suggested the war was lost.

Hitler's Delusions

The war was grinding to a halt. The Allies, who landed in France on June 6, 1944, fought their way east as the Russians pushed west, crushing Germany in between. Still, Hitler refused to admit defeat. He dreamed up elaborate counterattacks using divisions

of troops that existed only on paper or in his own mind.

On April 20, 1945, the top Nazis—Hitler, Göring, Goebbels, Himmler, Ribbentrop, and Speer—gathered in Berlin for the last time. Hitler ordered a final, all-out attack on the Russians. It never took place, and the Red Army broke through the outer defenses of the city. Hitler then resolved to turn over the conduct of the war to others and to stay in Berlin. According to General Alfred Jodl:

Hitler declared that he had decided to stay in Berlin, lead its defence, and then at the last moment shoot himself . . . for he could not run the risk of falling into enemy hands. We all attempted to bring him over from this decision. . . . His answer was that everything was falling to pieces anyway, and that he could do no more.[81]

Most of the top Nazi leaders had no wish to share Hitler's fate. They left their führer in his underground refuge and began to make their own plans for survival. Göring tried to take charge, but none of the generals would obey him; he was finally captured by American soldiers on May 9. After failing to make a private deal with the Americans, Himmler shaved his mustache, put on a private's uniform, and tried to escape the city. He was caught and arrested by British troops and, on May 23, killed himself with poison.

Hitler was enraged by what he considered the treachery of two of the men who had been closest to him. In his long, rambling final testament, dictated in the early morning hours of April 29, he expelled both from the party. He blamed everyone for the war and its outcome except himself. He had been forced into war, he wrote, by the British and French, and Germany had been defeated only by the treachery of the generals. In the final paragraph, the man who had brought such destruction on Europe echoed his life's dominant theme: "Above all I charge the leaders of the nation and those under them to scrupulous observance of the laws of race and to merciless opposition to the univer-

sal poisoner of all peoples, international Jewry."[82]

The Death of Hitler

Shortly before he dictated his testament, Hitler had married his longtime mistress, Eva Braun. In the early afternoon of April 30, Hitler said farewell to those who had remained with him, including private secretary Martin Bormann and the still-faithful Goebbels. He and his new wife then went into their room and closed the door. In a few minutes, a single shot rang out. When the others entered, they found the Nazi führer lying dead on a sofa, shot through the mouth. Beside him was the body of Eva Braun, who had swallowed poison. The bodies were carried up into the chancellery, placed in a shallow grave, doused with gasoline, and set ablaze. As the flames mounted, Goebbels and the others raised their arms in the Nazi salute.

Hitler and his wife, Eva Braun, committed suicide on April 30. Followers placed their bodies in a shallow grave and set them ablaze.

Hitler's Will

A few hours before he committed suicide in his underground bunker in May 1945, Adolf Hitler dictated a rambling final statement in which he claimed that he had been betrayed by the military and his closest advisers and lashed out once more at the Jews. Shortly afterward, he dictated a much shorter document, his last will and testament, quoted in Allan Bullock's *Hitler: A Study in Tyranny.*

Although I did not consider that I could take the responsibility during the years of struggle of contracting a marriage, I have now decided before the end of my life, to take as my wife the woman [Eva Braun] who, after many years of faithful friendship, of her own free will entered this town [Berlin], when it was already besieged, in order to share my fate. At her own desire she goes to death with me as my wife. This will compensate us for what we have both lost through my work in the service of my people. What I possess belongs—in so far as it has any value—to the Party, or, if this no longer exists, to the State. Should the State, too, be destroyed, no further decision on my part is nec-

essary. My pictures, in the collection which I have bought in the course of years, have never been collected for private purposes, but only for the establishment of a gallery in my home-town of Linz on the Danube. It is my heartfelt wish that this bequest should be duly executed. As my executor I nominate my most faithful Party comrade, Martin Bormann. He is given full legal authority to make all decisions. He is permitted to hand to my relatives anything which has a sentimental value or is necessary for the maintenance of a modest standard of life; especially for my wife's mother and my faithful fellow-workers who are well known to him. The chief of these are my former secretaries, Frau Winter, etc., who have for many years helped me by their work. I myself and my wife choose to die in order to escape the disgrace of deposition or capitulation. It is our wish to be burned immediately in the place where I have carried out the greater part of my daily work in the course of my twelve years' service to my people.

Days later, Goebbels followed Hitler's example. He and his wife, Magda, poisoned their six children and then took their own lives.

In the year following war's end, captured Nazi leaders were tried for crimes against humanity. The most famous of these trials was at Nuremberg, ironically the site of the party's greatest rallies. The twenty-two defendants included Göring; Hess; Ribbentrop; Hans Frank, Hitler's attorney and governor-general of Poland; Julius Streicher; Speer; Artur Seyss-Inquart, who betrayed Austria to the Nazis; and Franz von Papen.

Some of the defendants, including Göring, pleaded ignorance, claiming to know nothing about the death camps. Others protested that they were only following Hitler's orders. "Even with all this I know," Ribbentrop said, "if in this cell Hitler should come to me and say, 'Do this!' I would still do it."[83] Still others, like Streicher, were unrepentant, vowing they would do the same things if given another chance.

Shortly after 1 A.M. on October 16, 1946, Ribbentrop mounted the gallows in Nuremberg prison, to be followed by nine others. Göring, however, cheated the hang-man. Two hours before his scheduled execution, he swallowed poison that had been smuggled into his cell.

Only a very few of the defendants in the Nuremberg trials or any of the other war crimes trials seemed to be honestly sorry for the years of suffering and millions of deaths they had helped to bring about. One was Frank, Hitler's attorney and the brutal governor-general of Poland. He confessed his crimes and added, "A thousand years will pass and this guilt of Germany will not be erased."[84]

Who Was to Blame?

Terrible as it was, the Holocaust was not unique, only different in scope. The Nazis did not invent genocide. Sadly, the extermination of people for no reason except their membership in an ethnic group has darkened human history many times before and since.

During World War I the Turks drove almost 2 million Armenians into exile on a march during which about 600,000 starved to death or were killed by Turkish troops. Between 1929 and 1934, Joseph Stalin ordered more than a million kulaks, wealthy peasant farmers who resisted the seizure of their property by the Soviet Union, to be killed or deported to remote Siberia.

Many people vowed that the horrors perpetrated by the Nazis could never be allowed to happen again, but they have. Millions of people have been killed since World War II only because of their ethnic background—in Cambodia in the 1970s, in African tribal warfare in the early 1990s, and—even more recently, in Serbia, a part of the former Yugoslavia. In each case, mass murder was more than an experssion of hate. It was official government policy.

The Ultimate Crime

Why, then, does the Holocaust remain the example against which all other acts of genocide are measured? Why do the Nazis stand out as history's ultimate monsters, far more villainous than Stalin's secret police or the Khmer Rouge of Cambodia? First, the sheer enormity of the Holocaust is unparalleled. The number of those slain by the Nazis—estimated at more than 11 million—dwarfs all other examples. Second, the Holocaust marked the first time that the full resources of a modern, industrialized nation have been used for the express purpose of mass murder.

Third, the Nazis did not kill the Jews and other groups in the heat of battle, or to secure their property, or for any political goal. Instead, they killed Jews simply because they were Jews. Furthermore, they were not content merely to kill every Jew in Germany. Stalin had been concerned with the Soviet Union, the Serbs with Serbia, and the Turks with Turkey. The goal of the Nazis was to hunt down Jews wherever they lived.

Some scholars have argued that Hitler and the Nazis were freaks of history—that events and personalities merged in such a way as to bring about a unique phenomenon, one unlikely to be repeated. The problem with this conclusion is that the Nazis have reappeared, in different countries and with different names, but with the same

Jewish victims lie dead in a railroad car. The Nazi perpetration of the Holocaust remains one of the most horrible acts in history.

program of hate, racism, and genocide. In order to try to curb such reappearances, the questions must be asked: Who should have stopped Hitler? Who could have stopped him?

German Guilt

To a large extent, the entire German people shared the responsibility for the crimes their government committed. Hitler made no secret of his plans for the Nazi Party and for Germany. When he began to put those plans into action, only a few voices were raised in protest. The great majority of Germans either supported the Nazis, remained silent, or chose to ignore what was happening around them. Even many who lived within sight, sound, and smell of concentration camps claimed complete ignorance of their existence.

It is a mistake to think that the Holocaust was the doing of a small band of fanatics. To be sure, some of the Nazis were twisted, perverted monsters. The vast majority, however, were very ordinary people who found themselves in very extraordinary circumstances. Many were brutal and sadistic, but most viewed the mass killings as a job that had to be done. As much as the soldier on the fighting front, they longed for an end to the war so that they could return to their homes and families.

One of the most frightening insights into the Holocaust is that, far from being a small group of extremists, the Nazis were fairly representative of Germany as a whole. They came from all walks of life and, although the middle class was overrepresented, the membership of the Nazi Party was a reflection of German society.

In his book *Hitler's Willing Executioners,* Daniel Goldhagen studied a single unit, *Ordnungspolizei* (Order Police) Battalion 101, which engaged in mass murders in Poland. Most of the unit's 550 men were middle class; 42 percent were midlevel employees or civil servants. Only 179, 32.5 percent, were members of the Nazi Party and only 21 were in the SS. If Battalion 101 was typical, then ordinary Germans not only did not oppose the Nazis, but they also took as active and willing a role in the Holocaust as did party members.

One by one, Goldhagen cites the usual excuses for German participation in the Holocaust: They were afraid to refuse an order; they blindly followed orders; they felt intense psychological pressure to conform; they acted out of self-interest; and they did not realize the scope of what they were doing. He then demonstrates how each claim was largely untrue. He blames, instead, the Germans' unique tradition of anti-Semitism, their deep-seated belief that Jews were somehow subhuman. The Holocaust, he writes, came about "because of a set of beliefs which inhered [brought about] as pro-

found a hatred as one people has likely ever harbored for another."[85]

The German Defense

Certainly, this was not true of all Germans. Here and there, a few brave men and women spoke out against Hitler. Many more, however, who were disgusted by the Nazis, felt helpless to do anything and fearful if they

Scholars still debate the complex reasons that allowed the Holocaust to occur with little opposition. Although Hitler had devised the evil plan, it required the cooperation of the German people.

Supporters enthusiastically greet Hitler. Hitler appealed to Germans' nationalism, their resentment after World War I, and their economic desperation to help propel the Nazi Party.

tried. Author William Shirer recalled conversations with such Germans. "What could they do?" he wrote. "They would often put the question to you, and it was not an easy one to answer."[86]

The church was the social institution most likely to have led opposition to the Nazis. Indeed, many clergymen did speak out, including Reverend Martin Niemoeller, who in 1937 said, "No more are we ready to keep silent at man's behest when God commands us to speak."[87] Niemoeller and more than a thousand other pastors were arrested between 1937 and 1939 and languished in concentration camps until the war's end. Again, however, the great majority of church leaders bowed to Hitler instead of to God.

There were only two powers in Germany that could have stopped the Nazis: the industrial establishment and the military. Neither group particularly admired Hitler and his crude racial philosophies, but both were attracted by what the Nazi leader could offer them. The Nazis, he claimed, would restore both the German economy and the military to positions of world prominence after the shattering defeat of World War I. This was what the industrialists and the generals wanted to hear. They saw in Hitler the kind of strong leader they thought was needed. Their mistake was in thinking they could use the Nazis for their own purposes and then push them aside. Together, they must bear most of the blame for Hitler and the Holocaust.

Western Guilt

Outside Germany, the blame must be shared by the Western democracies: Great Britain, France, and—to some extent—the United States. Despite the warnings of a few farsighted leaders, such as Winston Churchill in Britain, the European powers bent over backwards to accommodate Hitler, giving him virtually everything he demanded in order to prevent a war. They had both the military might and the legal right to march against Germany when it sent troops into the Rhineland in 1936. What they lacked was the will. Instead, they stood by and allowed Germany's military to grow until it was strong enough to almost win the war the West wanted so desperately to avoid. The United States contributed indirectly to Hitler's success by withdrawing into isolationism after World War I, refusing to take a strong role in world affairs.

The most important task for present and future generations, however, is not to point fingers and assign blame, but to remember what happened in Germany from 1933 to 1945 and to learn from it. In this remembering and learning lie the best chances for preventing or halting future crimes against humanity. For, as the philosopher George Santayana said, "Those who cannot remember the past are condemned to repeat it." [88]

Notes

Introduction: Before the Storm

1. Quoted in John Weiss, *The Ideology of Death: Why the Holocaust Happened in Germany.* Chicago: Ivan R. Dee, 1996, p. 20.

2. Quoted in Weiss, *The Ideology of Death*, p. 23.

3. Quoted in William L. Shirer, *The Rise and Fall of the Third Reich.* New York: Simon & Schuster, 1959, p. 94.

4. Quoted in Klaus P. Fischer, *Nazi Germany: A New History.* New York: Continuum, 1995, p. 42.

Chapter 1: *Der Führer*

5. Quoted in Allan Bullock, *Hitler: A Study in Tyranny.* New York: Harper & Row, 1962, p. 27.

6. Quoted in Shirer, *The Rise and Fall of the Third Reich*, p. 12.

7. Quoted in Shirer, *The Rise and Fall of the Third Reich*, p. 13.

8. Quoted in Karl Dietrich Bracher, *The German Dictatorship.* New York: Praeger, 1971, p. 50.

9. Quoted in Fischer, *Nazi Germany*, p. 81.

10. Quoted in Shirer, *The Rise and Fall of the Third Reich*, p. 15.

11. Quoted in Shirer, *The Rise and Fall of the Third Reich*, p. 18.

12. Quoted in Bullock, *Hitler*, p. 36.

13. Quoted in Fischer, *Nazi Germany*, p. 88.

14. Quoted in Fischer, *Nazi Germany*, p. 90.

15. Quoted in Shirer, *The Rise and Fall of the Third Reich*, p. 26.

16. Fischer, *Nazi Germany*, p. 91.

17. Quoted in Bullock, *Hitler*, p. 40.

18. Quoted in Shirer, *The Rise and Fall of the Third Reich*, p. 22.

19. Quoted in Shirer, *The Rise and Fall of the Third Reich*, p. 27.

20. Quoted in Bullock, *Hitler*, p. 48.

21. Quoted in Bullock, *Hitler*, p. 53.

22. Quoted in Shirer, *The Rise and Fall of the Third Reich*, p. 32.

23. Quoted in Shirer, *The Rise and Fall of the Third Reich*, p. 35.

24. Quoted in Shirer, *The Rise and Fall of the Third Reich*, p. 38.

Chapter 2: Birth of the Party

25. Quoted in Louis L. Snyder, *Encyclopedia of the Third Reich.* New York: Paragon House, 1989, p. 297.

26. Quoted in Shirer, *The Rise and Fall of the Third Reich*, p. 48.

27. Quoted in Shirer, *The Rise and Fall of the Third Reich*, p. 40.

28. Quoted in Fischer, *Nazi Germany*, p. 125.

29. Quoted in Snyder, *Encyclopedia of the Third Reich*, p. 63.

30. Quoted in Bullock, *Hitler*, p. 69.

31. Quoted in Bullock, *Hitler*, p. 71.

32. Quoted in Bullock, *Hitler*, p. 82.

33. Quoted in Shirer, *The Rise and Fall of the Third Reich*, p. 89.

34. Quoted in Fischer, *Nazi Germany*, p. 154.

Chapter 3: Years of Growth

35. Quoted in Fischer, *Nazi Germany*, p. 160.

36. Quoted in Shirer, *The Rise and Fall of the Third Reich*, p. 77.

37. Quoted in Fischer, *Nazi Germany*, p. 161.

38. Quoted in Fischer, *Nazi Germany*, p. 162.

39. Quoted in Fischer, *Nazi Germany*, p. 163.

40. Quoted in Fischer, *Nazi Germany*, p. 169.

41. Quoted in Fischer, *Nazi Germany*, p. 176.

42. Quoted in Bullock, *Hitler*, p. 130.

43. Quoted in Shirer, *The Rise and Fall of the Third Reich*, p. 119.

Chapter 4: The Seizure of Power

44. Quoted in Shirer, *The Rise and Fall of the Third Reich*, p. 136.

45. Quoted in Shirer, *The Rise and Fall of the Third Reich*, p. 143.

46. Quoted in Shirer, *The Rise and Fall of the Third Reich*, p. 140.

47. Quoted in Shirer, *The Rise and Fall of the Third Reich*, p. 142.

48. Quoted in Fischer, *Nazi Germany*, p. 232.

49. Quoted in Fischer, *Nazi Germany*, p. 243.

50. Quoted in Shirer, *The Rise and Fall of the Third Reich*, p. 177.

51. Quoted in Otto Friedrich, *Before the Deluge: A Portrait of Berlin in the 1920's*. New York: Harper & Row, 1972, p. 381

52. Quoted in Friedrich, *Before the Deluge*, p. 382.

53. Quoted in Shirer, *The Rise and Fall of the Third Reich*, p. 198.

54. Quoted in Shirer, *The Rise and Fall of the Third Reich*, p. 201.

55. Quoted in Shirer, *The Rise and Fall of the Third Reich*, p. 216.

56. Quoted in Shirer, *The Rise and Fall of the Third Reich*, p. 217.

57. Quoted in Friedrich, *Before the Deluge*, p. 402.

58. Quoted in Fischer, *Nazi Germany*, p. 293.

Chapter 5: The Nazis and the Jews

59. Fischer, *Nazi Germany*, p. 390.

60. Quoted in Snyder, *Encyclopedia of the Third Reich*, p. 317.

61. Quoted in Yehuda Bauer, *A History of the Holocaust*. New York: Franklin Watts, 1982, p. 110.

62. Quoted in Bauer, *A History of the Holocaust*, p. 121.

63. Quoted in Shirer, *The Rise and Fall of the Third Reich*, p. 234.

64. Quoted in Snyder, *Encyclopedia of the Third Reich*, p. 268.

65. Quoted in Bauer, *A History of the Holocaust*, p. 118.

66. Quoted in Fischer, *Nazi Germany*, p. 392.

67. Quoted in Shirer, *The Rise and Fall of the Third Reich*, p. 431.

68. Quoted in Shirer, *The Rise and Fall of the Third Reich*, p. 432.

69. Quoted in Fischer, *Nazi Germany*, p. 393.

Chapter 6: War and Destruction

70. Quoted in Bullock, *Hitler*, p. 345.

71. Quoted in Shirer, *The Rise and Fall of the Third Reich*, p. 293.

72. Quoted in Shirer, *The Rise and Fall of the Third Reich*, p. 298.

73. Quoted in Shirer, *The Rise and Fall of the Third Reich*, p. 300.

74. Quoted in Shirer, *The Rise and Fall of the Third Reich*, p. 347.

75. Quoted in Shirer, *The Rise and Fall of the Third Reich*, p. 417.

76. Quoted in Shirer, *The Rise and Fall of the Third Reich*, p. 420.

77. Quoted in Fischer, *Nazi Germany*, p. 435.

78. Quoted in Fischer, *Nazi Germany*, p. 440.

79. Shirer, *The Rise and Fall of the Third Reich*, p. 743.

80. Quoted in Fischer, *Nazi Germany*, p. 469.

81. Quoted in Bullock, *Hitler*, p. 784

82. Quoted in Bullock, *Hitler*, p. 795.

83. Quoted in Snyder, *Encyclopedia of the Third Reich*, p. 296

84. Quoted in Fischer, *Nazi Germany*, p. 570.

Epilogue: Who Was to Blame?

85. Quoted in Daniel Jonah Goldhagen, *Hitler's Willing Executioners*, New York: Alfred A. Knopf, 1996, p. 389.

86. Shirer, *The Rise and Fall of the Third Reich*, p. 232.

87. Quoted in Shirer, *The Rise and Fall of the Third Reich*, p. 239.

88. John Bartlett, *Familiar Quotations*, 16th ed., s.v. 'Santayana, George."

For Further Reading

David A. Adler, *Child of the Warsaw Ghetto*. New York: Holiday House, 1995. Fictional account of life in the Warsaw ghetto, the uprising against the Nazis, and imprisonment in Auschwitz told through the eyes of a Jewish boy. Excellent illustrations by Karen Ritz. For younger readers.

Susan D. Bachrach, *Tell Them We Remember*. Boston: Little, Brown, 1994. Published for the United States Holocaust Memorial Museum. The entire story of the Holocaust, from the rise of the Nazis to the liberation of the concentration camps during World War II, told in short chapters liberally illustrated with photographs. Photographs of actual Holocaust victims and survivors are most touching.

Bruce Bliven Jr., *From Casablanca to Berlin*. New York: Random House, 1965. Simply written, easy-to-read account of World War II in Europe from the Allied landings in North Africa to the surrender of Germany. Relatively few photographs.

Edward F. Dolan, *Portrait in Tyranny*. New York: Dodd, Mead, 1981. Moderately difficult biography of the leader of the Nazis, Adolf Hitler. Text is well organized, but the clumping of all the photographs in a central section is awkward.

Sarel Eimerl, *Hitler Over Europe: The Road to World War II*. Boston: Little, Brown, 1972. Comprehensive account of the years from 1929 to 1939 covering the Nazis' seizure of power and the events leading to World War II.

Brendan John Elliott, *Hitler and Germany*. New York: McGraw-Hill, 1968. Excellent account of Hitler's rise and fall. Especially valuable in that it gives the background factors in Germany that made Nazism possible.

Albert Marrin, *Hitler*. New York: Viking Kestrel, 1987. Superior biography of Hitler for the more advanced reader complete with primary source quotations and a good variety of photographs.

Joshua Rubenstein, *Adolf Hitler*. New York: Franklin Watts, 1984. Volume in the Impact Biography series. Biographical account of the rise and fall of the Nazi leader. Good, moderately difficult text but short on photographs.

G. C. Skipper, *Death of Hitler*. Chicago: Childrens Press, 1980. Volume in the World at War series. Fictionalized conversation mars this otherwise good account of Hitler's final days. Outstanding collection of photographs.

———, *Goering and the Luftwaffe*. Chicago: Childrens Press, 1980. Volume in the World at War series. Excellent biography of Hermann Göring and the story of the buildup of the German air force and its attacks on Poland and Great Britain.

R. Conrad Stein, *Hitler Youth*. Chicago: Childrens Press, 1985. Volume in the World at War series. Simply written account with plenty of photographs of how the Nazis tried to take control of the minds of the children of Germany.

Richard Tames, *Nazi Germany*. London: Batsford Academic and Educational, 1985. A title in the Living Through History series. Short account of the Nazis' rise to power and minibiographies of the leading Nazis and some of their opponents.

Harold Cecil Vaughn, *The Versailles Treaty*. New York: Franklin Watts, 1975. Designed for the serious, more advanced student; a very thorough account of the treaty that ended World War I and its consequences, both immediate and long-term.

Works Consulted

Yehuda Bauer, *A History of the Holocaust*. New York: Franklin Watts, 1982. One of the world's foremost authorities describes both the Holocaust and the events leading to it. Charts and maps help the reader get an accurate picture.

Karl Dietrich Bracher, *The German Dictatorship*. Translated by Jean Steinberg. New York: Praeger, 1971. Very scholarly in tone and thus less accessible than some other accounts, but a very comprehensive examination of the Third Reich.

Allan Bullock, *Hitler: A Study in Tyranny*. New York: Harper & Row, 1962. A revised edition of a work first published in 1951, this remains arguably the best of all the Hitler biographies.

Klaus P. Fischer, *Nazi Germany: A New History*. New York: Continuum, 1995. An excellent and complete overview of the roots of the Nazi Party, its rise to power, and its destruction.

Otto Friedrich, *Before the Deluge: A Portrait of Berlin in the 1920's*. New York: Harper & Row, 1972. A good look at life in Germany during the early days of the Weimar Republic and the Nazis' rise to power.

Daniel Jonah Goldhagen, *Hitler's Willing Executioners*. New York: Alfred A. Knopf, 1996. Excellent study of how ordinary Germans, not only fanatical Nazis, were willing participants in the Holocaust.

William L. Shirer, *The Rise and Fall of the Third Reich*. New York: Simon & Schuster, 1959. Written by an award-winning journalist, this is one of the most comprehensive and readable histories of Nazi Germany.

Louis L. Snyder, *Encyclopedia of the Third Reich*. New York: Paragon House, 1989. An indispensable tool for anyone studying Nazi Germany. All the major people, places, and events are described in short articles in alphabetical order.

John Weiss, *The Ideology of Death: Why the Holocaust Happened in Germany*. Chicago: Ivan R. Dee, 1996. Explores the course of history in Germany and Austria and the character of their people in order to explain the Holocaust.

Index

Picture Credits

Cover photo: Corbis-Bettmann
AP/Wide World Photos, 15, 21, 42, 65, 73
Archive Photos, 64, 78
Archive Photos/Popperfoto, 52
Archive Photos/Potter Collection, 63
Corbis-Bettmann, 36, 46, 47
Deutschland Erwacht/courtesy of the Simon Wiesenthal Center Library and Archives, 26
Library of Congress, 13, 32, 34, 39, 51, 56, 76, 87, 88, 96, 97
National Archives, 18, 30, 53, 60, 81, 84, 86, 89, 90, 91, 95
National Archives, courtesy of USHMM Photo Archives, 48
Peter Newark's Historical Pictures, 40, 43, 49
Peter Newark's Military Pictures, 25, 82
Rijksinstituut voor Oorlogsdocumentatie, courtesy of USHMM Photo Archives, 71
Stock Montage, Inc., 57, 61, 66
UPI/Corbis-Bettmann, 16, 29, 69, 77
USHMM Photo Archives, 31
Yad Vashem, 79

About the Author

William W. Lace is a native of Fort Worth, Texas. He holds a bachelor's degree from Texas Christian University, a master's from East Texas State University, and a doctorate from the University of North Texas. After working for newspapers in Baytown, Texas, and Forth Worth, he joined the University of Texas at Arlington as sports information director and later became the director of the news service. He is now director of college relations for the Tarrant County Junior College District in Fort Worth. He and his wife, Laura, live in Arlington and have two children. Lace has written one other book in the Holocaust Library, *The Death Camps*.